THE
DUMBNESS OF THE GREAT

A Survey of the Nonsense, Absurdities, Inconsistencies, Illogicalities, Inaccuracies and Idiocies of the World's Outstanding Leaders

with a special bonus book

ABSURDITIES OF THE CHRISTIAN RELIGION

by

Joseph McCabe

THE BOOK TREE
San Diego, California

Dumbness of the Great
originally published 1948
E. Haldeman-Julius
Girard, Kansas USA

Absurdities of the Christian Religion
originally published circa 1936
Freethinker's Library

ISBN 978-1-58509-346-5

Cover layout & design
Toni Villalas

Cover art by Jacob Jordaens (1593-1678)

"The King Drinks"

painted circa 1640

oil on canvas

currently displayed at the Royal Museum of Art, Brussels

Published by
The Book Tree
P O Box 16476
San Diego, CA 92176
www.thebooktree.com

We provide fascinating and educational products to help awaken the public to new ideas and
information that would not be available otherwise.
Call 1 (800) 700-8733 for our *FREE BOOK TREE CATALOG*.

CONTENTS

PREFACE

We of the present day have, besides a solid pride in our scientific exploration of the universe and the triumphs of our applied science, the profound satisfaction of looking back upon thousands of years of ignorance. You might draw an analogy between man's slow and stumbling advance in the understanding of himself and the universe about him and the reading of a mystery novel. When civilized men first began to distrust their legends and traditions and make a direct inquiry into the nature of things they found themselves in a world of complete mystery. As time went on clues were spotted by sharp-eyed individuals and were developed a little in countries where the priests had not a monopoly of what they called truth. The first Greek inquiries guessed at the fact of evolution, the distance of the stars, the rule of law in nature, the atomic structure of things, the right of self-government, the absurdity of gods and goddesses, the social nature of moral law, and so on. But the clues were lost again or contemptuously thrust out of sight, and man plunged once more into the mist. As the race came nearer to the end of the book—to date—the clues stood out again and multiplied, and in our time we, comparatively speaking, see the clear outlines of the cosmic plot.

Even when we make full allowance for the inevitability of ignorance in earlier ages the guesses and statements of their oracles make up an entertaining volume. Who can fail to smile when he reads that doctors in ancient Egypt tried to stop the bleeding of a wound with a mixture of fly-dung and vinegar, that Plato believed we had recollections of an earlier life and Aristotle thought the heart the organ of thought and the brain just a cooling chamber, that according to Pliny elephants worship the moon, and St. Augustine insisted that the bones of the giant reptiles were the skeletons of the giants mentioned in the Old Testament? But we have serious reason also to recall these absurdities. Not only do ancient authorities like Moses, Jesus, and Mohammed still dominate the minds of half the race, but apart from religion many oracles of an earlier age still have their opinions thrust upon us. Some prate about the wisdom of ancient Egypt, and others praise the visions of Plato or Aristotle. Some 20,000,000 folk in enlightened modern America ask us to believe that Augustine or Thomas Aquinas stated truths for all time, while millions of others swear by Luther or Calvin, Washington or Jefferson, Karl Marx or Emerson. In a transitional age like ours, where the old and the new, the true and the false, mix in paralyzing confusion we have to learn to distrust all oracles of the past and realize that they lived in ages of such ignorance that even the eye of genius was astigmatic. We live in the most advanced hour of sunshine that the earth has yet known. Provided we set each of these old oracles in his particular stage of the progress of the race there is no harm in having an hour's entertainment with their guesses and absurdities.

I. ARISTOTLE AND THE ANCIENT WORLD

When the early Greeks marched down from the valley of the Danube and found civilizations across the sea which boasted of thousands of years existence they, in their recent emergence from raw savagery, naturally thought that there must be a superior wisdom in the Egyptian and the Babylonian. In those days knowledge was not obtained by careful observation and close examination of what you observed. It was either communicated by the gods or it was seen, in an inner mental light, by a few particularly gifted men or "seers." We know better; and since the priests of the older civilizations kept speculation in their own circle we look for no accumulation of wisdom in the old kingdoms. It is one of the absurdities we shall find in the 19th century that when the pressure of science was felt on old traditions a few mystic folk began to talk about the lost wisdom of ancient Egypt or Mesopotamia, of India, Thibet, or China.

The Greeks came upon the scene early enough to pick up and write in their books whatever wisdom had accumulated in ancient Egypt. Their famous traveler and historian Herodotus visited all parts of Egypt and wrote a lengthy account of it for centuries before it fell to the Romans. A great colony of Greek scholars and writers flourished in Alexandria a century later. In our own time the ancient tombs have been opened by the thousand, and in those hermetically sealed vaults we have found the toys with which children played, the cosmetics of their mothers, and the books that men read 4,000 to 5,000 years ago. We have a remarkable knowledge of what the Egyptians called wisdom, and it was on about the level of the European Middle Ages. For instance, a papyrus—the inner bark of a tree that they used as paper—dealing with medical "science" (though it was more of a black art) and going back to about 1500 B.C., one of the most brilliant periods of the monarchy, was found in a tomb in the ruins of Thebes. It claims a more or less divine knowledge of the art of healing and gives a number of prescriptions. King Teta gave this recipe for hair-oil to his mother when her hair began to fall: A mixture of asses' hoofs, dogs' claws, and dates, ground up and boiled and rubbed together in oil. To cure blindness you were to take two pigs' eyes and some eye-powder, vermilion, and honey in equal parts, rub them together and apply, uttering a magical formula, to the patient's ear. There is a lot of anatomy in the treatise and, though they had been cutting open and embalming bodies for ages, it was rudimentary. They had no idea of the circulation of the blood, and they thought that the blood-vessels, which they variously put at 10 to 40 in number, contained a mixture of water, air, and mucus.

One would have expected that one of the most pressing things they wanted to know was how to deal with the many diseases that plagued folk and carried them off prematurely—we can be sure that the average expectation of life was not much, if at all, over 20 years—in the densely populated valley, yet in 4,000 years they got little beyond the primitive belief that disease was due to evil spirits. The far greater part of the popular pharmacopeia consisted of spells and charms. Where a profane remedy was urged it might contain a real purgative or a useful food like honey, but it was generally a stupid mixture of useless and even loathsome stuffs. As I said, you stopped the bleeding of a wound with a mixture of fly-dung (which was very abundant) and vinegar. For a burn you mixed certain weird ingredients with some milk from the mother of a male child. Another recipe for baldness was a decoction of the hair of a black calf. You could tell whether a new born child would or would not live long if on the day of its birth it said Yes or No . . . But your safest bet always was to put your money on the priest and his devil-chasing spells.

What started the modern myth of the wisdom of ancient Egypt was the first close study of the great Pyramid early in the last century. We will take the assurance of Professor Breasted that in putting together this extraordinary pile of monstrous blocks of stone nearly 5,000 years ago the Egyptian displayed some knowledge of mathematics and considerable skill in stone-construction. That it shows a profound knowledge of astronomy is a myth, and the suggestion of a "lost art" of engineering has no ground. The Egyptian tradition was that the king employed 100,000 men for 20 years to raise this selfish monument to his glory, and we can easily visualize vast masses of men pulling and pushing the great stones up an inclined plane of sand and stone. We visualize at the same time a barbaric social system in which 100,000 men can be torn from their homes and driven by the lash to carry out that whim of an autocrat.

Some progress had been made in the direction of science. In the thickly populated valley there would be endless quarrels about the division of land, as a father left a plot to be divided amongst the sons, and long and tense experience had led to some development of elementary mathematics (arithmetic, mensuration, etc.). So with astronomy. Most profitable to the priests were the great festivals of the numerous gods and goddesses, and the fixing of a calendar by the movements of the heavenly bodies was a vital concern in the priestly colleges. But it stopped at practical use. Their idea of the universe was the familiar toy-theater picture: a vast dome of a solid firmament covering a flat earth of a few hundred miles in breadth and resting on solid walls or hills round its edges. A picture in one of the papyri shows how they thought the gods made it. In the beginning was a villainous old hag of a deity—the "deep" or chaos of Genesis I,2—and a handsome young god cut her in two with one sweep of his sword and made the heavens out of one half and the earth out of the other.

Out of thousands of years of experience in making pottery (later glass), dyes, and cosmetics—the ladies spent as much on these as modern girls do—they got an elementary knowledge of chemistry. But of what our mystics call the wisdom of the priests the less said the better. You read of a Book of the Dead (a modern name) as their bible, but the Old Testament is sober and sensible in comparison. It is the epic of the soul's journey after death through the perils of the underworld. Here is an average specimen (Book X, ch. 32):

"My soul arrives, it speaks with its father, saves the Great One from the Eight Crocodiles . . . Away, Crocodile of the West, who feedest on traveling [shooting] stars. What thundereth in thy belly? I have eaten the neck of Osiris. I am Set. Away, Crocodile of the West! The snake Nai is in my belly, and I will give it to thee . . . Away, Crocodile of the East, who livest on those that eat their excrements . . ."

They were not, as it used to be thought, a particularly religious folk—they were merry and fond of beer and notably amorous—but the priests hammered into them a terrific faith in devils, and no man can estimate what they spent on religion in the sense of devil-dodging. The only "wisdom" the old civilization has left us is a series of little moral treatises by middle-class men who smiled at the priests and their gods and devils—in some cases they were clearly Atheists—and worked out the rules of social life, even 4,000 or more years ago, much as we do today.

A discussion of Babylonia would run on the same lines, and I will make short work of it. A broad distinction between the two ancient peoples was that while the Mesopotamians did not believe in a future life of happiness or torture—all shades passed into a common misty underground that might be called oblivion—the Egyptians generally, after about 15,000 B. C., believed in judgment and a sort of paradise after death; though there was outspoken skepticism in the middle class, and the belief had no great influence on the gay life of the people. One result was that in Babylonia even more than in Egypt disease was attributed to demons, whom the gods let loose on men for their sins. Recent experts, however, consider that medicine was a little better developed in Babylonia than in Egypt, and there was the same development, under the stress of agricultural trade-requirements, of an elementary mathematics. The story of Herodotus, who apparently never visited this region, that the treatment of the sick was just to put the patient sitting in the street to ask passers-by for advice is one of those foreign libels (like the supposed custom of compelling every woman to prostitute herself in the temple) that the Greek picked up somewhere.

Astronomy advanced more than in Egypt. A Babylonian temple was, as everybody knows, a huge mound of brick more or less in the form of a pyramid and rising to several hundred feet. It had, like the Mexican *teocalli*, steps on the outside, and on the top was a little chapel with images, sometimes of solid gold, of the gods. From these, high above the dust of the plains, the priests contemplated a brilliant sky, and from the usual need to fix their calendar by the movements of the heavenly bodies they went on to get a good knowledge of the planetary system, though, of course, they kept the earth as its fixed center. But they made a more fateful blunder in putting deities in each of the heavenly bodies or in some vague way associating the gods with them. This easily led to a belief that the accident of your being born when one or the other deified body was "in the ascendant" influenced or predestined your whole career. This opened up to the priests a profitable business of forecasting, and astrology was imposed upon civilization for thousands of years.

Modern writers are not so ready to notice an even more costly blunder: the introduction into a popular book (or set of clay tablets), though it was not, like the Bible, regarded as a revelation, of primitive guesses at the making of the world and the origin and early history of man; of the stories of creation, Eden, the fall, and the flood which the Hebrews adopted. In no part of the world was there such an emergence of dry land from the waters as in Mesopotamia—the whole region was at first a watery swamp—and this seems to have inspired the idea of the creation of the earth and its trees and animals. Similarly a famous inundation, which we trace in the early Sumerian chronicles, prompted the story of a destruction of the race by water and survival of a favored hero in a boat. The primitive paradise and fall were, of course, attempts of the race in many lands to reconcile the miseries of life with the goodness of the gods. Babylonia took its legends lightly, but when the Hebrew priests turned them into a revelation civilization was burdened with another fatal outcome of "ancient wisdom." We shall see what a rich crop of absurdities arose when science came at last to discover the truth about origins.

The Assyrians, a cognate people, followed the Babylonians, and the fourth great civilization of the ancient Near East, the Persians, laid a more costly blunder than ever upon the race; though it is just on account of this contribution to the code and traditions of the race that they are still represented in our literature as the best of the pre-Christian nations. The blunders of Zarathustra, the half-mythical prophet of early Persia, have cost humanity far more than the mistakes of Moses. Some group of shaggy prophets on the Persian hills, which overlook the Babylonian plain, got hold of the idea of a primitive golden age and "improved" on it. The supreme and holy god had not, like Jahveh, made a fair and happy earth and then blighted it because men poached on the reserved orchard. He had created a world far more beautiful than ever the Babylonians or the Hebrews thought, because it was—though it included cows but not cow-dung or roast beef—entirely spiritual or immaterial. It was the supreme devil who, in his wicked jealousy, came along and turned it into a material world, giving man the body with all its lusts and its diseases. So life was a

7

fight of the spirit of man against his flesh, particularly his sex glands, and when the great god would one day tire of the sport and burn the terrestrial theater, he would judge all men and send them either to heaven or to hell.

Naturally the great majority of the Persians took no more notice of the theory, which they called their religion, than medieval folk took of their version of it. The only conspicuous change in Persian life when they became civilized was a large spread of sodomy. But the asceticism of the theory appealed to the founders of Christianity and it became part of the official creed of Europe. Even today men and women who have realized the absurdity of paying any attention to the old Babylonian legends still cherish the ascetic deductions from the Persian myth and complicate the human task. We shall see the absurdities with which they defend their positions later.

In the 7th century B.C., when this pregnant myth seems to have been born in Persia, the world was ripe for new ideas. Civilizations that were 3,000 years old were sinking under the blows of invaders or from internal decay and dissension, and new and vigorous peoples like the Greeks and Romans were coming on the scene. In point of fact, as we now see, a new era—an era of real inquiry and independent thinking— was opening, and it might have become the Modern Era if it had not been for the long blight and reaction that followed the triumph of Christianity in Europe and Nearer Asia. Its outstanding oracles were found to blunder, for they had no large basis of accurate knowledge, and, after a glance at Asia, I will briefly show how the new movement culminated in the absurdities of Plato and Aristotle, since they are still forced upon us as the wisest men of the old world.

In Asia, as is known, Buddha and Kung-fu-tse (or Confucius) appeared in the same age. Of Kung, in China, I need say only that he is the one oracle or prophet of the ancient world in whom we find no serious absurdity or inconsistency. He was so firm and clear-headed an Atheist that his ethic was never turned into a religion; though, since it is the prevailing fashion still to say that there can be no high ethic without religion, Confucianism is absurdly described in our literature as one of the world's four great religions. It is just a code of social behavior.

In India, which was 2,000 years older than China as a civilization, conditions were different. The ancient Hindu religion had sunk to the level of the peasants, and the robust nature-religion of the Aryan invaders had become one of the most abstract metaphysical religions ever invented. The priests put together long strings of words that seemed sometimes to have lost all meaning. Opening one of their sacred books at random I read:

"There are a hundred and one arteries of the heart; one of them reaches to the crown of the head, and moving upward by it a man reaches the immortal . . . That which is the subtile essence in it all that exists has itself. It is the true. It is the self."

This sentence is repeated in chapter after chapter as a profound truth. In the highly esteemed *Mahabbharata* we read such things as this:

"The ear, the skin, the two eyes, the tongue, the nose, the two feet, the two hands, the speech, the genital organ, and the anus, these verily are the 10 sacrificial priests. Sound, touch, color, taste, smell, words, actions, motion, and the discharge of seed, urine, and excretions are the 10 oblations."

The educated laity rebelled against this sort of futility and by the 7th century had a widespread school of atheistic philosophy. Buddha was reared in this school and, while he was always faithful to its Atheism, in the ascetic group of disciples that he gathered about him he spoke a slightly mystic language which in time helped the degeneration of his system into a religion.

But the main interest for us is in what happened in the West at this important turn of world-history. I have in so many of my books insisted—because in general literature it is almost ignored—on the historical importance of the strip of Asia Minor that faces the Aegaean Sea, which the Greeks called Ionia, that here I will be brief. In the great and beautiful cities of Ionia the Greek immigrants intermingled with the merchants of the older civilizations and, being free from the tyranny of Greek or any other priests, turned to the direct study of nature and life. There is no doubt that they were greatly helped by the astronomy of Babylon and possibly by the science of the Phoenicians. A series of middle-class merchants thus founded what was called philosophy but was really science, besides forming a sound social code of conduct. When the Persians captured the cities the disciples of these men scattered over Greece and South Italy and, with sometimes fantastic variations, continued to develop their views.

All the works of thinkers of this Ionian school and all but one— the work of the Roman poet Lucretius—of the works of the Epicurean school which succeeded it were destroyed in the flames of Christian vandalism, and historians of philosophy warn us to distrust the opinions attributed to them by Greek rivals. That these men uttered many absurdities goes without saying. They lived in the dawn of thought. But they claim our special sympathy for two reasons. They did discover truths of such fundamental importance and so rich in suggestion that science would have revealed its power ages ago if the race had persevered on the Ionic line of thinking. I would, in fact, venture to say this: By the year 1000 of the present era, when Europe had sunk back into barbarism, it would have reached the pitch of knowledge and power that we have today, and we of today would be many centuries ahead in the growth of civilization, if these Greek beginnings of science had been steadily developed. To see this one has only to reflect on the fundamental principles they formulated. They discarded all beliefs that gods created the universe and said that it was the outcome of an evolution of an eternal matter. They said that matter consisted of atoms, which was the basis of the great chemical advance of the last century. They guessed that the sun was the center of the solar system, the earth a globe, and the stars large bodies at an immense distance. They said that gods and spirits, if there were any—Epicurus said, rather as a concession to ignorant bigots, that there might be gods, who knew no more about men than men knew about them, in some remote part of the universe—had nothing to do with the affairs of man or the phenomena of nature; and they accordingly stated a high social-moral code of conduct of a purely humanist character.

The second point is that even the extravagances of the early pioneers represented scientific speculation without the check of creeds or authority. For instance, to explain how so orderly a world arose out of a jostling of an infinite number of atoms they had to say that if you imagine these atoms mixing in an infinite space during an infinite period they must run through every possible combination, including the ones we see. This lends itself to absurd suggestions such as that man's eyes, toes, kidneys, etc., were formed separately before they were united in man. The greatest thinker of the series, Democritus, corrected this by saying that the conjunctions of the atoms were not by chance in the ordinary sense; that the universe was ruled by law. But he seems to have been vague about the nature of this law, and at this point the mystic school arose.

Some said that the difficulty was surmounted by supposing that there was "mind"—a material and impersonal mind—in the universe, and just then the mystic ideas of the later Egyptians and Persians reached the Greeks. There seems to have been a sort of religious revival amongst the people at the time, and the political or social pressure of fanatics is always dangerous in a democracy and is apt to be felt even in the cloistral study of the philosopher. At all events an entirely new strain of thinking began with Pythagoras, in the Greek colony of South Italy, who made a glorious mixture of late Egyptian mysticism and mathematics. It says much for the thoughtfulness of the Greek world

9

that, as was the experience of most of the Greek thinkers, he at once secured a large body of adherents and was, unlike modern philosophers, a prominent figure in public life. But there are absurdities that are not amusing and I will not waste space on those of Pythagoras. As Professor Eric Bell says: "Only the mentally incompetent are impressed by any of this meaningless mysticism today."

Meantime the argumentative sculptor Socrates at Athens had taken up the idea of "mind" in nature and had insisted that this must be a personal spiritual God. He had the good fortune to convert the most gifted of Greek prose writers, Plato, and he, blending the ideas of Socrates with the Pythagorean doctrine of the spirituality and immortality of the soul, gave the world what is called the first great spiritual philosophy. His was a strange genius. His proofs of God and the soul —he even believed in transmigration and said that we had recollections of our earlier lives—were rhetorical and sentimental, yet he was the first sociologist and had fine, if occasionally eccentric, ideas of social and legal reform.

But instead of giving here a string of the absurdities and eccentricities found in his writings I prefer to emphasize the mischief of his fundamental or spiritualist idea. In his rhetorical fashion—in personal life he was not at all ascetic—he exalted the value of the spiritual above the material as much as did a Persian dervish or a later Father of the Church. This material world is just a heap of muck. Anything good or beautiful that you see in it comes to it, as the light reaches it from the sun, from a better world: a world in which the Good, the True, and the Beautiful are at the same time—in a sense nobody has ever understood—both ideas and realities. Matter is contemptible, a study of it a deplorable waste of time. He even wanted the works of all the Ionian thinkers burned.

Naturally in the Christian era he was saluted as a great thinker, and the modern world has not yet shed its medieval illusions. In the Greek world of his time he had a mere handful of followers, and his still greater (from the intellectual point of view) pupil Aristotle rebelled against his fundamental ideas. In a freer age Aristotle might have become the greatest of the early pioneers of science and rendered a mighty service to the race. But in the previous generation the Athenians had condemned Socrates, a firm believer in God, to death, and other philosophers had had to fly for their lives. The Athenian democracy was still bigoted, and it seems to me that this had more to do with the semi-mysticism of Aristotle than Plato had. He knew all the science of his time and did a good deal of personal observation and guessing. At one time Alexander the Great paid him $400,000 to make inquiries all over the Greek world and Asia and write a "History of Animals." If you care to read the inevitable absurdities of such books of 2,000 years ago you will find lots of passages like these:

Some animals have their teats in the breasts: others between the thighs.

Straight-eyebrows indicate soft manners: those that curve toward the nose are an austere person: those that curve toward the temples a derider and dissembler.

Man's higher and lower parts are arranged according to the higher and lower parts of the universe.

The brain in all animals has no blood or veins and is cold.

In the larger animals the breath reaches the heart through the veins . . . the veins convey hot air from the lungs to the heart (and cool mucus from the brain to it).

If the eyes of serpents are dug out they will be reproduced . . . the salamander shows that some animals can live in fire.

Fat and suet are different: fat does not congeal.

Nightingales have been seen teaching their young to sing.

All testaceous animals (oysters, etc.) are generated spontaneously in the matter which is at the bottom of the sea . . . land-molluscs in the crevices of rocks.

Large numbers of insects are generated spontaneously . . . in putrid mud or dung or rotting wood or in the hair, flesh, or excrements of animals . . . caterpillars are born spontaneously in green leaves . . . Eels are generated from the entrails of the earth or spontaneously formed in mud and dry earth.

Bees do not make honey: it falls from the air, mainly about the time of the rising of the stars and when the rainbow rests upon the earth.

The menstrual purgation of women takes place at the waning of the moon . . . Snakes are friendly with women and suck their breasts.

Those whose knees are so close together that they nearly knock against each other are sodomists.

Mutilated children are born from mutilated parents.

He did not even believe that the brain had anything to do with thinking, as others claimed. He, it is true, made personal contributions to the slender natural history of the time, especially in relation to sea-shore animals, but this rather shows a preponderant interest in sex-matters. The popular idea that he was a cold-blooded intellectual worker·is absurdly wrong. Disraeli says in his "Curiosities of Literature" that he "joined to a taste for profound erudition that of an elegant dissipation" or a fine taste in mistresses and choice foods.

With this—for the time—encyclopedic knowledge of science and his great intellect—no man ever had a greater—he might have impressively promoted the advance of knowledge but, as a high authority has said, all his work is weakened by the conflict of his scientific and his obscurantist or metaphysical bent. Like almost all the Greek thinkers he rejected the idea of spirit as an absurdity, but he put in its place the idea of the immaterial: something (like man's mind or soul) that did not come from matter yet could not exist apart from it. His physics and astronomy were spoiled by this tendency. He rejected the atomism of the Ionians and thought that it was enough to say that every object in nature had a "form" which gave it its qualities. He rejected their idea of evolution and could think of nothing else to say about origins. His argument for a God as Prime Mover of the universe (the usual flat-earth with an over-arching vault) was fantastic, though it is still used in Catholic philosophy, and his persistent looking for "ends" or purposes in things led him constantly astray. For instance, the path of the sun, moon, and planets round the earth *must* be circular because the circle is the perfect figure.

In short, he introduced the illusion of affecting to study nature in the light of reason or first principles instead of direct observation. If the Greek world had followed him, the development of science both in Alexandria and in the medieval Arab world and modern times would have been far slower and less fertile, and we should not be where we are today. It is, in fact, a platitude of the history of science that the adoption of Aristotle as almost supreme by the medieval Arabs and Schoolmen, on account of his complete opposition to Materialism, caused the professors of philosophy in the universities to resist and hinder science almost as fiercely as the theologians. That was the monumental blunder and disservice to the race of one who is still presented to us as the greatest thinker of all time.

Fortunately the Greeks were too mentally alert to be seduced by either the iridescent spiritual writings of Plato or the severe semi-spiritualism of Aristotle. Neither had more than a handful of followers, and only for a short time. With Epicurus the Greek world returned to the Materialism of the Ionians, and just at that time the Greeks built the city of Alexandria, a new area free from priestly domination, and the great colony of scholars there carried mathematics, physics, astronomy, and medicine to a higher stage. Men were still groping in the half-light of dawn, but they were straining to make a study of realities not consisting of some imaginary inner light. Crude as it seems in com-'

11

parison with our knowledge, the following account of the origin of things from Diodorus Siculus, a geographer of the 1st century B.C., will show that they were headed in the right direction:

"When the universe came together in the beginning of time the heavens and the earth, these elements being nearest together, had a common form. Then, as these bodies moved away from each other, the world came to have the shape in which we now find it, though the air continued in a state of perpetual agitation and the fiery part of it rose to the greatest altitude because its lightness causes it to rise. So the sun and the rest of the heavenly bodies were involved in this whirl. But the thicker elements of the air, mixed with moisture, settled in a lower position on account of their weight . . . It formed the sea out of the moist elements and the earth out of the more solid, though the earth was at first muddy and soft. It began to harden under the rays of the sun. Then the surface began to swell and ferment on account of the heat in many places and raise some sort of blisters with skins, as happens now in marshes and ponds. When these humid places were "fertilized by heat, as if by genital seed . . . at last the membrane burst and the forms of animals appeared (Geography I, 7)."

About the same time Lucretius, who gives all this also, was saying: "Man's first weapons were his fingers, teeth, nails, stones, and sticks. Later was the age of iron, but it was preceded by one of bronze." The race was getting into its stride.

II.   AUGUSTINE AND THE CHRISTIAN FATHERS

There are two kinds of absurdities perpetrated by men of high intelligence. One is the crude guess at the nature of things which is inevitable while knowledge is scanty. Men of an earlier age would pardon us for being amused at these things, and we recognize the inevitability of them and are grateful that they broke out avenues of inquiry instead of bowing to authority and tradition. Science had to begin that way. A different kind of absurdity is that of one who permits a creed or philosophy to make him defy existing knowledge or distort it into harmony with such creed or philosophy. It is important to remember the distinction. It is possible that some propositions which we stoutly hold today will seem amusing to another generation, but if they are statements that are made after severe inquiry and with mind unhampered by any traditional belief we shall be forgiven. It is far otherwise with those who obstruct the advance of knowledge in the name of some alien interest. It is, in fact, of great importance to us to realize how that advance of the race in real knowledge which substantially began with the Ionian scientists and has proved such a rich source of power and enlightenment in our time has been repeatedly and for many centuries held back in the interest of philosophy or theology. We want to identify these forces.

The first such obstruction to man's advance in that knowledge of himself and his world that is the indispensable basis of human welfare we have seen. In the name of "spirit," which is just the sublimation of a superstition of primitive man, certain scholars of Athens either scorned outright (Plato) all study of nature or pretended to find an inner light or power of intuition which was superior to reasoning upon what one saw. Fortunately the little influence they had perished when they died, and it was the materialistic ideal of the Stoics and Epicureans—indeed, almost entirely of the latter—that impelled the Greeks from 300 B.C. onward to develop and expand the science of the Ionians. This was chiefly done in Alexandria, an island of culture where neither the priests of Egypt to the south nor those of Athens across the sea, could dictate in the name of their legends.

The Romans added practically nothing to the sum of human knowledge. Lucretius finely expressed the creed of the Epicureans, and Pliny gathered together the scattered and amusing fragments of "natural history" much as Aristotle had done. His work abounds in such gems as:

"Eels originate in what are called the bowels of the earth and are found spontaneously in mud and moist earth.

· "On the approach of a woman in the menstrual state milk turns sour, seeds which are touched by her become sterile, garden plants wither . . . her look blunts the edge of steel . . . A swarm of bees, if looked upon by her, will die immediately.

"Elephants are so intelligent that they do homage to the moon . . . so modest that they always mate in secret, and only on five days every other year, when they purify themselves . . . Adultery is unknown among them . . . They live to be 200 or 300 years old."

The earth, he says, is 1/26th part of the entire universe, of which it is the center, and stretches from the Pillars of Hercules (Gibraltar) to India. The moon is the nearest of the stars:

"It is rightly believed to be the star of the breath, and it is this star that saturates the earth and fills bodies at its approach and empties them as it recedes. Shell-fish and all animals with blood, increase in size as it approaches and animals die only when the tide ebbs . . . this is true at all events in the case of man."

But already the mathematicians, astronomers, and close observers of Alexandria were correcting these illusions. They proved the sphericity and the approximate size of the moon and the sun, and were building up a picture of the universe.

But by this time there had appeared in the Greek-Roman world a force which was destined to extinguish the new aspiration of men to understand themselves and the universe around them and to plunge the human family back into barbarism: the force which nearly every oracle in America now assures you opened the founts of wisdom to men, created a higher civilization, and is so indispensable a basis for the maintenance of that civilization that we ought to blast the cities of unbelievers with atomic bombs and drench their country with poison gas and poisonous germs.

I do not propose here to examine the absurdities and extravagances —the belief in the devil and hell, the coming end of the world, the malediction of wealth and comfort, the sour condemnation of sexual pleasure, and so on—that are attributed to the gospel Jesus or the additional monstrosities—original sin, bloody atonement, etc.—of Paul, but to glance at the contortions into which the Fathers or leaders of the church were driven by their blind obedience to the largely mythical books of the Jews and of Christianity. Most of these bishops were men of no learning. The Roman see had not a single bishop with the knowledge of an ordinary Roman gentleman during its first 400 years and no Pope of real learning for nearly 1,000 years. Most of the other "Fathers" were little better but, as we should expect, it was impossible for them to be indifferent to learning in the city of Alexandria. Here the early leaders were Origen and Clement, and Catholic literature glows with admiration of their prodigious learning.

As I said, they could not afford to be indifferent to learning in a city like Alexandria, which had succeeded Athens as the cultural metropolis of the world, but their only interest in it was to convince the Greeks that it could be brought into harmony with the fantastic statements of the Christian books. Origen, one of the early Christians who castrated himself in virtue of a text about eunuchs in the New Testament, might be called the Father of Modernism; and he was correspondingly suspected of heresy. He began the figurative or allegorical interpretation of the Bible. You just turn an inconvenient text inside out and prove that a writer of 2,000 years earlier really anticipated the discoveries of the learned Alexandrians if you read a deep symbolism into everything. The Alexandrians smiled when, for instance, they read about Jesus riding into Jerusalem on an ass. They had heard the same about the jolly god Bacchus. But the gospel story, Origen said, was just a symbol of the new religion coming to men on the back of the Old Testament.

Clement sustained the good work. Abraham's three-days' journey to Mount Moriah was a symbol of the three stages of the soul's progress in knowledge of God. The mention of three Hebrew towns in Isaiah was really a forecast of the three Wise Men who visited Jesus in his cradle. The barley loaves and fishes of one of the miracles of Jesus symbolized the preparation of the world for Christianity by the Jewish Law and the philosophers. Does not barley ripen before wheat? And was not philosophy born in the waves of the pagan world just as the fish are in the sea? But the harvest was poor amongst the educated Greeks, and church leaders in happier (or more ignorant) regions did not like the idea that God, in dictating the scriptures to their writers, concealed his meaning until learned Greeks came along and discovered truths which enabled you to see what he really meant. Ought these explorers of the guts of the earth, these frivolous guessers at the structure of the heavens, to be mentioned in the same breath as the word of God? Were not the whole of their attempts to discover the nature of terrestrial things a wilful waste of time that ought to be spent in thinking about God?

So the plot to strangle the infant science in its cradle was woven. Until the 4th century this was of no more practical consequence than the stupid assaults on modern geology of the Seventh Day Adventists or the ravings of Father Divine. As I have shown elsewhere the orthodox claim still pressed upon the general public in American papers by Catholic writers who pay the paper instead of being paid by it, that the new religion swept the Roman world, is as fabulous as the Age of Chivalry. At Rome, for instance, they shivered amongst the social outcasts outside the city—they had not even one small chapel until the year 222—until the Emperor Constantine became a semi-Christian and they were let in and dazed with a shower of gold. They had, as groups, never been conspicuous for virtue, and their ascetic minorities now shrank more than ever. The clergy became numerous, rich, and sensual—read St. Jerome's scorching description of them and their "holy virgins"—and one might expect that, if there were any truth in the modern claim that the church always was the patroness of learning, they, or a few of them, would cherish the Roman world's slender inheritance of it. The historical truth is different. It was just at this stage that the general and virulent contempt of science began. And this was not from asceticism, which was so rare that St. Jerome says that if you met an obviously ascetic woman in the streets of Rome you said: "There goes a Manichaean," a deadly heretic. It was because-knowledge was, is, and always will be as fatal to all clerical bodies as our modern insecticides are to smaller parasites.

Lactantius, tutor of the Emperor Constantine, and the best educated Christian of his time, led the campaign. He took up and intensified the saying of that other "learned" Latin Father, Tertullian, that "after Jesus Christ all curiosity, after the gospels all inquiry, are unnecessary." As proof of the stupidity of these explorers of the universe he quoted some of them who had realized that the earth is a globe and said that there might be men on the other side of it or at the antipodes. With fine scorn he asks:

"Is there anyone so senseless as to believe that there are men whose footsteps are higher than our heads or that the crops and trees grow downward?"

Constantine's chaplain, Bishop Eusebius, who was the second most accomplished Christian (and smoothest courtier) of the time, said:

"It is not from ignorance of the things they (the pagan scholars) admire but from contempt of their useless labor that we think little of these matters and turn our souls to better things."

Eusebius's successor Basil repeatedly has the same scorn of research. He says of the great Greek investigators:

"Endowed with a penetrating mind for vanities they become deliberately blind when it is a question of knowing the truth. They measure the distance of stars . . . With all their resources of observation only one thing escapes them . . . the discovery of God, the creator of the universe."

Jerome, the finest Latin writer in the church, is just as scornful about the study of literature. Ambrose, the famous Bishop of Milan, the best-educated (in pagan schools) Christian of his time and in his pagan days Governor of a province, is just as bad. I need not quote the more ignorant bishops and will sum up the campaign in quotations from Augustine.

But it is necessary to note first that the ravings of these leaders of the church extended to far more of life than the acquisition of knowledge. From the same root came their contempt of marriage and of women. They follow Paul's disdainful concession that "it is better to marry than to burn" (in hell). Jerome said with the same disdain of weaklings: "I praise marriage because it produces virgins," and in his letters to aristocratic Roman young ladies he draws pictures of the inconveniences of matrimony in coarser language than any novelist dare or would use today. "Evangelical chastity," he says in another letter "will cut down the forest of the law and of marriage." They knew that they could not get more than a few of the Greeks and Romans to share their loathing of the sex-act, in or out of marriage, and they concentrated, with supreme contempt of social interests, on forbidding divorce or a second marriage. Athenagoras fairly put the feeling of most of them when he said that "marriage is only a decorous sort of adultery." A second marriage, even when a man's wife died, was worse. It was not even plausibly decent. Even in this, however, human nature in the faithful was too strong for the zealots and it was not for another seven centuries that the church could suppress divorce.

But while the assault on marriage and divorce failed, this contempt of sex, which easily extended to contempt of woman, had grave consequences for women which lasted for 1,500 years. In the old feminist movement in America a dozen women gave in their books the sordid opinions of their sex in the Fathers, yet the clergy easily persuade women today that the Church was always their best friend. St. Gregory Naziazen who was considered the most tender and emotional of the Fathers, said (in poetry):

> Fierce is the dragon, cunning the asp
> But woman has the malice of both.

Tertullian wrote a book on "The Adornment of Women." He told them that if one of them realized "her condition as a woman" in the Christian religion she would "dress in rags and remain dirty as a sorrowful and repentant Eve." "Thou art the devil's gate" he says to her, "the betrayer of the tree, the first deserter of the divine law." The learned Clement of Alexandria said that "it brings shame to a woman even to reflect of what nature she is." Gregory Thaumaturgus said: "You might find one chaste man in a thousand men but not one chaste woman in a thousand women"; and the great Ambrose said that "it becomes not the modesty of a maid to choose a husband." St. Augustine wonders in his commentary on Genesis why God made women at all and can suggest only that it was in order to make the fall of man certain. Jerome thought the only use of her was to help "those who are afraid to sleep alone at night." And all these poisonous absurdities, for which woman was to suffer bitterly until the 19th century, were perpetrated by men who are now represented as moral prophets who uplifted civilization, because the Jews had turned into a sacred oracle and misrepresented, out of anti-feminist prejudice, an ancient Sumerian fable about the fall of man. In the Babylonian version the man is not tempted by the woman. She was a man's equal in Mesopotamia and Egypt.

On many other points also the social code was distorted instead of improved. These Fathers began the condemnation of taking interest on a loan that lasted more than 1,000 years and was endorsed by all the great theologians of the Middle Ages. "Money," said Basil, is "a fecund monster." "Let us cut off these monstrous births of gold and silver; let us stop this execrable fecundity," said Chrysostom. But how could one expect a sound or sensible code of social conduct from men who despised almost all that it was the function of social life to provide for the citizen?

In fine, history was as grossly treated as science. Having a Bible that was full of supposed history they could not abolish it so they loaded it with lies and fictions. Again it was Lactantius and Bishop Eusebius who set the ball rolling as soon as the end of the persecutions left them free to walk the streets of Rome; like colored folk in Richmond after emancipation. Lactantius, who as imperial tutor and librarian had the best sources of information, at once wrote a work, "On the Deaths of the Persecutors," which is a classic of mendacity and the source of half the fables about the early church. It runs in this wise:

> "In Nero's time Peter came to Rome (which the Roman Christians of the 1st century denied) and by performing miracles by the power of God he converted many . . . And when this was brought to the ears of Nero, and he saw crowds not only in Rome but everywhere abandon the cult of idols and embrace the new religion, he set out to destroy the heavenly temple . . ."

He says that Nero in the end just disappeared and will reappear with Satan on the last day. Bishop Eusebius, the "Father of Ecclesiastical History," was equally fluent when it served his purpose; which was, he says, to edify not to instruct the reader. He it is who says that Constantine was converted because before his last battle a cross appeared in the heavens with the words "Conquer by this" (not "In this sign shalt thou conquer"). He says that the emperor, with whom he was intimate, told him so. Constantine was a brute, the murderer of his wife and son, but Eusebius was a more accomplished liar. Within a century Christian writers were turning out forged lives of saints and martyrs, teeming with absurdities and anachronisms, by the thousand.

All these absurdities found a culmination in the later works of Augustine. In order to understand how Catholic writers can quote quite respectable sentiments from the works of Augustine you must know that he had a good education in pagan schools, and for years after his conversion he remained a fairly refined student of the Platonic philosophy. But years of work as a bishop steeped him with the opium which he served out to his ignorant folk and he became extraordinarily credulous and desperate in his attempts to square existing knowledge with his faith. Catholics—even some scientific men of the appeasing school—often quote him as a pioneer of evolution because he said that God had merely put "the seeds of things" into the soil of the world. The truth is that in a later Commentary on Genesis he stuck out sourly for a literal interpretation, and in a work that he called "Retractations" he damned every liberal sentiment he had ever professed. He opened the game of "reconciling science with the Bible" which was to last to our time. At one point he denounces "the delirious elucubrations" of astronomers and says:

> "We refuse to make subtle research on the size and distance of the stars: to waste time that could be given to more important and better subjects."

He had not, incidentally, the slightest qualifications to make astronomical research, but the fact is that he uses science to support Genesis. The Bible says that God made a firmament dividing the upper from the lower waters. We saw that the earlier Greek speculators did suppose that the blue arch was a solid structure resting on a wall or a range of hills round the edge of the earth. Augustine grasps at this—it supports the "upper waters" that trickle down sometimes (in rain)—and scornfully rules out the finer work of the later Greek astronomers. These upper waters, he suggests, explain why Saturn moves so slowly. It passes through them. So man's primitive and childlike conception of the universe was imposed upon Europe, in the name of the Bible, for another 1,000 years, and all the brilliant work of the Alexandrian astronomers was lost. And he imposes also the absurdity of astrology:

"It would not be impious to say that the heavenly bodies are not without power on the external variations of bodies."

He means on anything that happens to us and is not an act of free will. Commenting further on the first chapter of Genesis, which has inspired a volume of absurdities that would fill the basin of Lake Michigan and has massively obstructed the progress of science, he says:

"I confess that I do not know why mice and frogs, flies and worms, were created (Luther later suggested that the devil created flies to distract us when we read the Bible.) As to the hurtful creatures, we are either punished or disciplined or terrified by them so that we may not cherish a love of this life."

Some, reflecting on the wide distribution of animals over the earth, had had doubts about the flood, but that is easy to Augustine. He imagines legions of angels ready at Mount Ararat to bear the elephants, rhinoceroses, tigers, etc., back to their jungles when the waters ran down the sewers:

"It cannot be denied that the transfer may have been accomplished through the agency of angels, commanded or allowed to do this by God."

In fact, there are proofs of the flood. Even in those days quarrymen occasionally came upon the bones of the Mesozoic great reptiles. When a find was made in his district Augustine explained to his wondering flock that these were the bones of the human giants mentioned in Genesis! They were drowned in the flood. When the story of God taking six days over his job troubled others Augustine fell back upon the rubbish of Pythagoras:

"There are three classes of numbers—the more than perfect, the perfect, and the less than perfect, according as the sum is greater than equal to, or less than the original numbers. Six is the perfect number. Therefore we must not say that six is the perfect number because God finished all his work in six days but that God finished all his work in six days because six is the perfect number."

In another place he takes up the extensive amours of the early patriarchs, which scandalized some. "They acted from a sense of duty not a feeling of lust," he assures his readers. Well, he was asked, if the procreation of children is so important and a man's wife is barren, may he experiment with a concubine, as the Lord told some of these holy patriarchs to do? Augustine, the great moralist, gives it up:

"It was lawful to the patriarchs; whether it is lawful now or not I should not like to say."

In short he endorses all the absurdities of the early Fathers and carries through the tendencies of their principles so resolutely that one of his Catholic biographers, Nourisson, says of his moral philosophy:

"Taken literally and in certain pronouncements, though these are usually episodic and have been abused, his teaching destroys liberty of conscience, justifies slavery, shakes the foundation of private property, reduces history to special pleading, enthrones theocracy, and at the same time, in various respects, discourages toil and love of glory, transfers the march of civilization, and paralyzes the energy of all science, especially of the physical and natural sciences."

17

And this French philosopher is wrong only in the reserves he makes. For instance, while it is notorious that Augustine fully supported the persecution of unbelievers, it is not so well known, though it may be read by any man in his greatest work, "The City of God" (Bk. XIX ch: 15) that he defended slavery and declared that God had instituted it because of the sins of men. He says:

"The first cause of slavery, then, is sin—that one man should be put in bonds by another; and this happens only by the judgment of God, *in whose eyes it is no crime.*"

As to the charge that he "discourages toil," which may not disgust but will certainly surprise the reader, it is a correct reference to Augustine's work "On the Work of the Monks," one of his worst incoherencies. He gives a scorching account of the morals of the swarms of monks who now began to roam over Europe and plainly shows that the parasitic life attracts lazy hypocrites from all parts. Then he concludes that the monastic state is holy and must be encouraged, and he actually forbids the heads of the communities to inquire into the qualifications and character of those who demand admission to it. I commend the work to those (if they can read Latin) who imagine, from reading modern Catholic literature, that it was Benedict who first formed communities of monks, and that the monasteries were oases of peace and virtue for men who fled from a violent and vicious world. Benedict in the introduction to his Rule repeats and amplifies Augustine's shuddering description of the morals of the vast majority of the monks of his time.

Catholics, who are accustomed to present Augustine in their literature, as the wisest leader and most profound Christian thinker since Paul—the greatest leader that arose in the church before Thomas Aquinas, if not a greater than Thomas—would be embarrassed by the above quotation from a Catholic and expert writer if they ever reproduced it. They are today, and especially in America, not as honest as they were at one time, though honesty was never their chief virtue. My own biography and study of Augustine (1903) was published also in America and was on the reading list for students of history in Columbia and other universities. I doubt if you will find it today. Augustine has to be represented like Aquinas, as so serene, sound, and inspired an oracle that he can be taken as guide even in our age It is the very cream of absurdity. All the Fathers despised "the things of this world," but Augustine, who lived at the time of the fall of the Roman civilization, was worse than any. The aim of his chief work. "The City of God," was to convince folk that this collapse of their civilization did not matter. All the splendid achievements of Rome were not worth bothering about. All the things that make up what we call a high civilization are at the best concessions to the weakness of the flesh and concern about them is a distraction. One thing only matters: an ascetic preparation for the mythical life beyond the grave.

III. AQUINAS AND THE SCHOOLMEN

The monument to the memory of Augustine and all the absurdities, incoherences, blunders, and inhumanities of him and the other Fathers was the Dark Age. In St. Paul's cathedral at London there is an inscription on the wall that says to the visitors: "If you seek his (the architect's) monument look round you." Europe in the Dark Age was Augustine's monument, for he was taken during the next seven or eight centuries as its supreme architect. If you look for literary absurdities in the past you might dump in almost the whole literature of the next eight centuries. And you will have to be an expert to know anything about it. Who, except a dry-as-dust professor, or a theologian, ever reads any book that was written between Augustine's "City of God" (A.D. 413) and Dante's "Divine Comedy" 900 years later. The only other book

that has any circulation is a small collection of "love letters" of Heloise
—those of Abelard (after castration) that are strangely coupled with
them are as bleak as those of Augustine—and are a defiance by an
abbess of the Christian ethic. As to the great works of Aquinas (13th
century) not one priest even in 1,000 ever reads a line of them. It is
the same with science and, for six centuries, art generally. And there
are professors of history in American universities who, to please the
Catholics, tell you that there never was a Dark Age!

I say that you might include the whole literature of the eight centuries after Augustine in a gallery of absurdities but we are here concerned with the blunders of men who are recommended to us as great
or learned. How many such can you count, from memory, in those
eight centuries, which were *not* a Dark Age? Probably only Abelard;
and he was twice solemnly condemned for heresy and is known to you
only because he was castrated, by order of a canon of the cathedral, for
a love-affair. Catholic writers will tell you that your ignorance is due
to the world-prejudice against or jealousy of the glories of their church:
that in the centuries after Augustine there were learned writers, even
on science like Bede, Isidore of Seville, Alcuin, Rhabanus Maurus, and
Pope Silvester II. There were, as a fact, a few more brilliant men than
these (Scotus Erigena, etc.) but they were, of course, heretics so the
Catholic does not mention them. As to the men he does mention, they
do little more than repeat the worst blunders of the early pioneers of
science and of Augustine, but I may give a few words about them.

It is necessary to understand what happened to the culture of the
old world. Briefly, it all went up in Christian smoke, an offering of in-
cense to the new Almighty. Under pressure from the bishops the emperors ordered that all pagan temples must be closed or destroyed. Philis-
tines as all these Christian emperors were—brutes in many cases—
they did not want the destruction of the finer temples, which were
museums of art and had libraries attached. But local bishops and monks
led the mob against them with axe and torch. The burning of the great
Library of Alexandria with its 700,000 books—it is a medieval legend
that only a small part of it was burned—symbolized the death of the
old culture. A few Roman Christians wrote little manuals of such fragments of science as the Fathers had been able to distort into conformity
formity with the Bible, and these were used by the more prominent
writers whom Catholics quote to redeem the "honor" of the Dark Age.
During the reign of the heretic king, Theodoric, who did not bow to the
Popes and wanted to restore the old civilization, these fragments were
collected by Cassiodorus and passed on to the next generation. In the
Greek half of Christendom, where there was not the excuse of a barbaric invasion, an Egyptian monk, Cosmas Indicopleustes, who had
the repute of being a great traveler, put together a picture of the universe from the crude older astronomy that had been corrected by the
Alexandrians, and it was within this narrow frame that everything was
confined. Cosmas's map was used by the few scholars. It showed a flat
earth—he violently opposed the idea that it was a globe—about 400
days journey (say 4,000 miles) across, overarched by the solid firmament, above which were the vast cisterns that slopped over when it
rained, and the plug of which had been pulled out by Jehovah in the
days of Noah.

Bede and all the others accepted this. Bede was the abbot of a
monastery in the north of England and as credulous and narrow-minded
as he was pious. A century ago he was unknown outside the church.
In our kindly age he is one of the cultural heroes of the Dark Age. His
chief work was a church-history of England, in which he explains
that, the Picts, who came from Scythia (!), joined the British and had
a great civilization in the island, which—he lived in it, remember—is
"almost under the North Pole." In pre-Roman times it had "28 noble
cities besides innumerable castles," and it had hot-water springs, which
he explains by the fact that "water is heated and boils when it passes

near certain metals." Doubtless now that I have discovered this passage Catholics will claim that there were then large beds of uranium in the north of England and Bede knew all about it.

The ecclesiastical part of his history probably draws upon existing records but it is full of fables as absurd as his suggestion, to confound skeptics about the flood and the floating zoo, that Noah spent 100 years building the ark, that God administered (or sent the angels with hypodermics) an anesthetic to the animals when they were all aboard so that they would require no food for the duration of the flood (which brilliantly refuted those pagans who had asked about the storage of the food-supply), and that after all half the animals of the world were born by spontaneous generation (see Aristotle) and parents would not need to be taken into the ark. And so on through the early centuries of the Christian Era, when miracles were as common and as easy to grow as mushrooms, and martyrdoms were hourly events. In his own day, he says the monasteries and nunneries positively scented the air with their fragrance. As baths had died out with the Romans there doubtless was some sort of aroma round them in summer, but as to virtue we have the contemporary assurance of a more intelligent saint than Bede, St. Boniface, that English nunneries were then gay brothels for the "nobles" and the nuns even murdered the babies they bore.

You know what to expect when the purblind monk gets to science. He brilliantly suggests that the firmament is probably of ice; which explains how it can bear a great burden of waters yet be transparent. (The English had then no glass.) His explanation of earthquakes and tides is picturesque:

"Some say that the earth contains the (biblical) animal Leviathan, and that he holds his tail after a fashion of his own so that it is sometimes scorched by the sun. Whereupon he tried to get hold of the sun, and thus the earth is shaken by the commotion of his anger. He sometimes also drinks in (the ebb tide) such huge volumes of the water that when he belches them forth again the seas feel the effect (flood tide)."

Amongst other legends which he lodged in the English mind until the islanders became wicked and skeptical in the 19th century was that of the Dead Sea. Where the wrath of God had fallen nothing could live in the sea, no bird could fly over it, and, while beautiful apples grew in the gardens round it, they turned to smoke and ash (Dead Sea fruit) if you plucked them. Another idea that he stamped deep for centuries was that "comets portend revolutions of kingdoms, pestilences, wars, storms, or heat." They are exhalations of fiery air like the gas you see over a marsh and are lit by sparks dropping from above. And so on.

Probably that will be enough of Bede for you. But the great Isidore, Archbishop of Seville, is not much better. Since the Papacy discovered, almost the other day, that science is not really the spawn of the devil but the offspring of Catholic wisdom, Isidore has been growing larger and larger. The notice of him in the Catholic Encyclopedia tells you that he knew Greek and Hebrew as well as Latin and had a profound thirst for knowledge. On the other hand, a work on him published by Columbia University, which—to put it mildly—is not anti-Catholic, shows that he knew neither Greek nor Hebrew and was interested in science and history only to be able to prove how they confirmed the Bible. One of his summaries of history illustrates this:

"Joseph lived 105 years: Greece began the cultivation of grain (which was in full cultivation thousands of years before there was a Greece). The Jews were in slavery in Egypt 144 years: Atlas discovered astrology. Deborah lived 40 years: Apollo discovered the art of medicine and invented the cithara."

He says that the earth is flat and "circular," but he is hopelessly confused as to whether that means that it is a globe or a round flat plain. The four heavens—he has the usual wedding-cake picture of the universe—correspond to the four elements. The uppermost storey is, since fire is the lightest of the elements, the bright or fiery heavens, from which sparks (shooting stars) drop and comets' tails are fired. Below that is the air-sphere, in which angels (hence their wings), birds, and demons (the Spirits of the Air) live. The third down is the water-world (the reservoirs of heaven), and the fourth is earth. Above the top of the cake is the Christian Olympus, surveying the theater. The stars are bright lights that God rivetted in the solid firmament. The sun's motion is due to the rapid whirling of that region, and the moon takes eight years to circle the earth. Tides are probably due to the fact that there are big holes like nostrils in the floor of the ocean, sucking the water in and blowing it out, but some point out how these tides coincide with the waxing and waning of the moon. He leaves that difficulty to God, but he accepts the old story that bodies on earth wax and decrease with the moon.

On natural history he has all the amusing old stories:

"Deer are enemies of snakes, and when they feel themselves sinking from weakness they draw snakes out of their holes with the breath of their nostrils and eat them.

"Lions rub out their tracks with their tails, so that the hunter cannot find them.

"There are whales with bellies the size of mountains."

The latter sentence shows him deducing natural history from the Bible (the story of Jonah), but as a rule he follows the worst of the old stories. On one point he is original. He is great on etymology as a guide to truth. Beaver, for instance, is in Latin *castor*, and the animal is so named because it castrates itself when it is cornered and eats its testicles, which are good fighting medicine. Female whales copulate with muscles. The reason for this amazing and original absurdity is that the Latin word musculus is much the same as masculus (a male). He introduces into European tradition such fables on the swan's song ("a very sweet song"), the eye of the eagle which can look straight into the sun, and so on. In man the heart is the seat of thought (a mixture of Aristotle and the Psalmist), the arteries convey air from the lungs to the body, a man weeps when he kneels because that posture brings his knees and his eyes close together . . . But that will do for this blazing paragon of learning. He was more intelligent than most of his sensual and boorish colleagues in the gross Spanish kingdom of the Visigoths but Catholic writers who laud him to the skies absolutely ignore the brilliant civilization that the Arabs set up in the same city, Seville, two or three centuries later. A force of 10,000 Arab horsemen had knocked over the whole vast kingdom of these Visigoths in a few months like a castle of cards built by a child.

The monk Rhabanus Maurus was just another of these compilers of pearls of ancient wisdom rubbed up with biblical powder and need not be quoted; and Alcuin, the British monk who went as literary adviser to Charlemagne does not call for more than a few words. The ancient legend, still set forth in full in Catholic literature that he was a prodigy of learning who helped Charlemagne to cover his kingdom with a network of schools was demolished by scholars 100 years ago. It is true that Charlemagne ordered the gay-living bishops and abbots to open schools, but there is no evidence that they did, and all authorities on the history of education are agreed that if any more were opened they were promptly closed when Charlemagne died. They are further agreed that Charlemagne got much more help from a Lombard anti-Roman cleric whom he brought from Italy. We have still the writings of Alcuin. Besides small works on grammar and rhetoric they are just theological treatises in which the usual astronomic absurdities of the earliest pioneers are made to confirm the scriptures. The earth is a flat plain surrounded by four oceans. Beyond these are the mountain-bases on which the walls that support the firmament and stars rest . . . Such was "the Restorer of Science in the West."

The truth is that what Catholics falsely represent as a flare of social idealism in the kingdom of Charlemagne—a boorish sensualist whose "greatness" has been severely debunked by modern historians—lit by a representative (Alcuin) of a flourishing British culture blinds the reader, as usual, to the real cultural development of Europe. For a time after the Christianization of England and Ireland some of the hundreds of new monasteries devoted themselves to study. They had small libraries of a few hundred books, mainly theological—the Romans before them and the Arabs soon after them had thousands of libraries rising to hundreds of thousands of books in some—and their "culture" was as I have described it in the case of Bede and Isidore. The real line of development, which the Popes consistently opposed, was that first the "barbarian" Ostrogoths tried to restore Roman culture in north-central Italy, and then the (at first) equally barbarous and anti-Papal Lombards really effected a creditable revival in the same region. It was from the Lombard cities that Charlemagne got his real help. But the Church ruined his hesitating attempt, as it ruined both the Ostrogoth and the Lombard civilization, and Europe sank deeper into barbarism.

The situation is even worse when we find the Catholics boasting of Pope Silvester II as not only the first "great Catholic scientist" but actually a scientific Pope. Not only was such scientific knowledge as Silvester (or Gerbert) had of purely Spanish-Arab origin but he had been educated in Spain. Catholics generally say that he merely went to Christian Barcelona, which was part of Catholic Spain though Arab in culture, but the leading modern authority on him proves that he studied in Cordova, where he left unfragrant memories. The Arabs say that he seduced the daughter of his Muslim host and stole the chief treasures of his library. His contemporaries significantly say that he had a passion for collecting books but was never known to ask for a work of one of the Fathers. In any case his writings, which are mostly theological, occupy only 50 pages in the Migne edition. His fame rests entirely on rumor in Rome, which was then so low that the "noblest ladies" could not sign their names. In fact, there is ground to believe that the clergy upon whom he was imposed by a romantic young German emperor poisoned him off in three or four years and he left nothing but hatred behind him.

It would be tedious and, in fact, would require a volume, to tell all the absurdities that were written in these centuries, yet I may remind the readers, briefly, that this was just the period (say, 900 to 1300) when science made its greatest advance before modern times. This was in the Moslem, or Arab-Persian, and largely skeptical civilization of which I have written repeatedly. It is treated with gross disregard by modern historians generally because it was plainly the splendor of that skeptical civilization—it was reactionary wherever it was really religious—that at last quickened some intellectual life in Europe. These are points upon which I cannot enlarge here. I have done so elsewhere. It will be enough to say that it started a school-movement in the Christian countries of Europe which in the 13th century developed into the busy university or Scholastic movement of which Thomas Aquinas, Albert the Great, and Roger Bacon were the chief figures. We will dismiss the latter two shortly and concentrate on Thomas, whom Catholic writers still press upon the world as the Aristotle of the Middle Ages, a man so profound that his writings offer guidance for all time.

Of Roger Bacon it is enough to say that his scientific bearing has been recognized for more than half a century as purely Arab. The poor friar was kept imprisoned, mostly without books, pen, or paper, during most of his monastic life. It seems clear that he had a great capacity for science but was allowed no opportunity to do more than write down what he had learned in the school of Arab science at Oxford. He had no influence and no successors.

Albert, or Albert the Great, on the contrary, was a Dominican monk but of noble family and could not be pushed about like a poor Franciscan friar. The only sort of muzzle the church could put on him was to make him a bishop, when his zeal for science evaporated. It is generally held that before that he had made some personal research in botany but otherwise most of his science was the sort of stuff of which I have given many samples. Occasionally he rejected the more absurd stories—he denied, for instance, that birds are formed from trees by spontaneous generation and live on sap—but admitted such weird nonsense as that you could raise a whirlwind by dropping a certain salve into a spring, that both good and bad spirits (and witches) flew through the upper air, that they caused storms, that thunderbolts are formed in clouds that contain a good deal of mud baked by the sun, and so on. A special absurdity of his was to attempt to explain things by the verbiage of Aristotle, which was introduced into Europe by the Arabs. In other words, he selected the weakest point of the Arab philosophers, the cult of Aristotle, and helped to enthrone his authority, with disastrous consequences to science, in the universities of Europe. For instance, what we call fossils had by this time become familiar. To the Fathers they were the bones of victims of the flood. Albert grandly explained—and some such explanation held the field and blocked geological explanation for centuries—that they were just oddities formed in the rocks by a "formative" or a "lapidific" force. Albert in turn had no successors and no influence on the development of science. Two friars had attempted to kindle an interest in science. The church at once closed upon their monastic bodies and forbade them to pay attention to science.

THOMAS AQUINAS

But we will pay more attention to Thomas Aquinas (1227-74), not only because Catholics insist that this is the great oracle for all time but also because he wrote on many different subjects and we need not here confine ourselves to statements that are absurd in science. Friar Thomas—he was a Dominican monk, a man of such monstrous belly they had to cut a semicircular piece out of the table to accommodate it —came from South Italy, while Sicilian-Arabian science was well known and the memory of the great skeptic Frederic II was still fresh. He had a smattering of such knowledge before he settled in Paris, and for a time he was a pupil of Albert. But there was not the palest shadow of skepticism about Thomas. He swallowed every article and detail of medieval theology as you swallow an oyster, gave them, with the help of what he understood to be Aristotle's philosophy—it was late in life when he got a fair translation—the severe and pretentious form they still have, and made an organic whole of that pseudo-scientific form of religion which we call theology.

His absurdities in that field I do not propose to notice. To his wondering age he made angels and devils seem as natural as butterflies and beetles. Eternal punishment, he showed, was so logical a punishment of sin that God could not do otherwise. God is infinite: therefore the guilt of sin is infinite: therefore the punishment must be endless. The stream of verbiage flowed out with the smoothness of Lippmann's essays or Winchell's assurances. The incarnation and bloody atonement were as natural as a snowfall. Miracles, the resurrection, the application of fire to damned souls, the nature of the eternal joy of paradise, etc., he took in his stride. He swallowed to the last full stop the whole mendacious history that the Church had forged for itself since Peter, and all the crudely forged documents on which it based its temporal as well as spiritual power. The trinity was as easy as arithmetic . . . He was, the Catholic submits, the greatest genius that ever lived and could have made our Edisons and Einsteins look like fools.

All this meant that Aquinas fastened on the mind of Europe with bonds of iron, until the blacksmith Luther came along, those claims of power which the Popes had gradually fabricated. The spiritual power is the sun and the temporal or civil power the moon, so there was no question as to which was superior. He had not the slightest shade of doubt about the serene justice of the vile actions of Innocent III (Massacre of the Albiginsians, foundation of the Inquisition, treachery to Frederic II, etc.) in his own century. Burning men for heresy was as just as the rules of chess.

"It is much graver to corrupt the soul than to corrupt the coinage, which serves only to meet the needs of the body. Hence if coining and other crimes are justly punished by death by secular princes how much more ground there is not only to excommunicate heretics but to put them to death.

"The spiritual life is better than the corporal. But we put to death murderers who take the life of the body so we are all the more bound to kill heretics who take away the spiritual life of man . . . It is just that the secular courts should put them to death and confiscate their property *even though they do not corrupt others,* because they blaspheme against God and observe a false faith. It is more necessary to punish them than traitors or coiners . . .

"On no account shall the church allow infidels to have power over the faithful or to be set above them in any way . . . The church is above the state . . . kings must be subject to priests."

These arguments are still used in the Public Law (kept in Latin, of course) of the churches, as reprinted in the 20th century and taught to selected priests, including Americans, from all over the world in the Papal University, and American Catholic apologists lie about it. Aquinas was unquestionably a man of gifted mind but, quite honestly, he used his intellectual power to give the most impressive form and, apparently, a massive foundation of reason and morality to the gross imposture and fabric of forgery that the Popes of the Middle Ages built up. This is the real Aquinas that American priests and foreign refugee Catholics like Maritain urge upon the American public as one of the greatest thinkers of all time and a fit oracle for today. The above sentiments are found over and over again in his works and are still the sentiments and principles of the church, reaffirmed against Mussolini as late as 1929.

It may seem curious that a mind so steeped in theology and so instinctively credulous should write, besides his enormous "Summary of Theology," a volume of philosophic argument, supposedly based upon pure reason, for God and the soul against skeptics. If you ever read the poet Dante you will know why. A great respect for the skeptical Arab philosophers, Ibn Roshd (Averroes) and Ibn Sind (Avicenna), had spread in Christendom. But Aquinas' arguments are just the logic-chaffing of Aristotle's metaphysics further weakened to make them proof of a personal God and personal immortality in which neither Aristotle nor the Arab philosophers believed. These absurdities you may read in "Catholic philosophy" today.

More interesting is what Thomas says about social and political questions. He is as dogmatic a defender of autocratic monarchy as of the devil or the Inquisition. Some Catholics say that on the political side he merely translates Aristotle. He does not profess this but does in the main translate Aristotle—with the monstrous addition that the church is above the state—because he agrees with him. Other Catholics say that since Republicanism was unknown in Thomas' day this is quite natural. But Thomas, who surely knew well the recent history of his own church, was fully aware that the Romans had fought the Popes for 200 years to get self-government in a Roman republic and that the struggle had ended in a victory of the Popes, by treachery and violence, less than a century earlier. In any case, there was one profound difference between Aristotle's and Thomas' defense of autocracy. To Aristotle's purely utilitarian arguments Thomas added that kings got their authority from God, and that was the great bulwark of absolutism in Christendom for the next five or six centuries.

In the special work "On the Rule of Princes" and in a letter to or short treatise written for the Duchess of Brabant Aquinas has other profoundly mischievous and reactionary sentiments. He is emphatic that woman is rightly excluded from public life. Her place is the home. He, following Augustine, justifies slavery. It is, of course, entirely false that the church ever condemned slavery, but Catholics are particularly careful to suppress the fact that their supreme social and political oracles, Augustine and Aquinas, defended it. There is a book in French by the distinguished Belgian lawyer E. Crahay on "The Politics of St. Thomas Aquinas" which gives full quotations from Aquinas on these points and the exact references. The author is a Catholic, and it is "rather in sorrow than in anger" that he gives these points. He quotes:

"Those only form part of the civil community who are united in a life of virtue. For if it were for the mere sake of living that men joined in a communal life, animals and slaves would be part of the civil community.

"That man is naturally a slave who has a natural aptitude to depend upon another, in the sense that he cannot rule himself by his own reason, which is the gift that makes man master of himself but only by the reason of another; he is, therefore naturally the slave of another."

So far he more or less follows Aristotle's moral blunder but in other places he endorses that of Augustine and declares that slavery is, by divine appointment, one of the consequences of original sin.

He blunders just as badly in regard to another of the comprehensive crimes of the Middle Ages that the church complacently sanctioned: the vile treatment of the Jews. The Duchess of Brabant (Belgium) had consulted the oracle about the morality of confiscating the property of the Jews, which was done everywhere. It is entirely just, he tells her:

"Since the Jews are according to the law sentenced to perpetual slavery for their sins the rulers of the countries in which they are found may seize their property, provided that they do not deprive them of the necessaries of life."

What a sublime concession!

I have translated the passages given here directly from Thomas' Latin words. You will know now what to think of the effrontery of propagandists who offer him as an oracle for our time. What blunders he made, incidentally, on the scientific side it is hardly necessary to tell. He endorsed all the current absurdities and fables. He knew nothing of the splendid progress the Arabs and Persians had made in astronomy, and so he not only adopted the wedding-cake idea of the universe but accepted astrology in lots of texts.

"It seems to me that there is no sin in using the judgment of the stars to predict natural evils, such as stormy or good weather, health or sickness, abundance or poverty."

He endorses the superstitions of sailors, accepts the current view of comets, and approves of surgeons who consult the stars before operating. Choisnard quotes him saying:

"The heavenly bodies are the causes of what happens in this world, and experience has shown that by observing the stars we can foresee certain future events."

The Chaldeans had had a certain logic in their astrology, as they believed that a deity of specific character was associated with each planet. The whole logic was knocked out of it when you rejected the idea that Mercury, Mars, or Saturn was in the ascendant when a man was born. According to Thomas it was not these ancient deities but angels that caused the movements of the planets; I am almost tempted to say, pushed them along their appointed paths.

In spite of the brilliant progress made by the Arabs in physics—the basis of the invention of the telescope—and chemistry Thomas clung to Aristotle's absurd theory that you understood things by supposing

25

that each was compounded of "matter" (not as we now take the word) and "form." Water had a form, aquosity, which explained its properties, the plant a vegetative "form," the animal an animal form, and so on. Large numbers of animals were "produced by putrefaction." The forces in man—intelligence etc.—were quite independent of his structure and only to be studied by the philosopher and the theologian . . . The reader will smile when I say that, as professor of philosophy in a Catholic seminary, I was solemnly teaching this absurd matter-and-form theory 50 years ago. As far as I can discover it is still taught, and it is the "scientific" basis of the weird doctrine that in his mass the priest converts bread and wine into the real, full, living body and blood of Christ!

So we leave what the Catholic calls the greatest thinker of history. His works are a supreme example of "the dumbness of the great" in the sense in which I use the expression. They show, however, how a mind high above the average can be narcotized and stultified by Catholic doctrine, and that every writer who presses Aquinas upon the attention of the modern world must falsely represent his ideas and carry the policy of suppression to the point where it is equivalent to mendacity.

IV. LEADERS OF RENAISSANCE DAYS

What we now call the Renaissance, a period (in Italy) of about 1100 to 1500 (to 1600 in France, Spain, and England), is the time when Europe was recovering the lost arts and culture of civilization. It was a period of a remarkable artistic efflorescence, which does not concern us in this book. But the splendid color of the period obviously means a great advance in the creation of wealth, and this implies the rise of a large middle class and an extensive literature. Here then, since knowledge was still scanty and even moral sentiments were perverted by theology and in many respects as rudimentary as in Aquinas, we have a happy hunting ground for absurdities. If you reflect for a moment, however, you will probably find that you can hardly name a single writer (before 1500) in whom we might look for "the dumbness of the great." If you care to look into the matter you will in fact find that apart from artists, poets, and story-writers this brightest period of the Middle Ages was singularly poor in great men; and we do not examine the work of poets and story-writers (Dante, Chaucer, Petrarch, Villon, Boccaccio, Poliziano, Ariosto, Michael Angelo, etc.) for absurdities. There were no "great Popes"; and Frederic II, who had not time to write books, was the only great ruler. In short, there was a superb amount of splendid art, a terrific ferment of life, a vast amount of literature, and mighty little thinking on serious matters. And that must seem a paradox to those who have read in our modern sophists that the school-movement of the 13th century had fully awakened the intellect of Europe.

It might seem a deeper paradox if you are aware how from 900 to 1300 the Arabs and Persians, which means quite as many people and as much territory as there were in Christian Europe, had really cultivated the mind as well as art and beauty, and had made considerable progress in every branch of science and literature. But if you know that you probably know the solution of the paradox. In a word, it is the Inquisition, the tyranny of the church over the intellect. A truthful historical picture of the period is Rembrandtesque. It blazes with color, art, adventure, and love: it is dark as hell, red-relieved by slow-burning fires, in respect of serious literature. You could paint pictures or carve statues that a modern cop would pull his hat over his eyes to remove to the crematorium. You could write verse, comedies, essays, or stories that would give our modern censors apoplexy, though they made Popes and cardinals of the time rock with laughter. But they all professed a profound respect for the assurance of Aquinas that a heretic was worse than a murderer and must be put to death.

One of those complaisant American professors who are too amiable to offend anybody, even a Catholic, explains why he slights the great Arab civilization of 900 to 1300. It was not really great, he says. It had no great painters or sculptors—he forgets that the Koran strictly forbade the painting or carving of human or animal forms—it frittered chemistry away into alchemy, astronomy into astrology, and so on. Now this is, as far as science is concerned, a correct picture, not of the Arab but the Christian civilization of the Middle Ages. Every prince, lay or clerical, had his astrologer to direct his movements or detect plots for him; but astronomy made no progress from the last Arab expert to Copernicus. Every bishop had his alchemist to find the elixir of life or the philosopher's stone (which would turn base metals into gold) for him; but the few real chemists had to work underground. The only free science was medicine, as even the bishops and popes wanted to keep out of heaven as long as possible, but it did not even remain at the high level of which the Arabs had carried it. As a result the kind of absurdities about nature and man of which I have quoted so many had their life prolonged for a few further centuries, and what we might call the moral absurdities, or perverse opinions about standards of conduct, were worse than in Aquinas. For all its glamor of silk and gold, its beautiful buildings and glittering courts, it was in many respects (banditry, cruelty, torture, treachery, violence, and injustices) still a savage age, and the church's sex-ethic was never more blatantly defied.

But since this is a work on the absurdities of "the great" this will be a short chapter since, apart from artists, there were no great. How the old errors still dominated the mind of Europe is well shown by the popularity of a book by an English friar, Brother Bartholomew, on, as he said, "The Properties of Things." It was greatly esteemed all over Europe during the whole period; and remember that the mass of the people (or almost nine-tenths of every nation) still could not read, so that those who admired it were merchants, officials, lawyers, clerics. As a matter of fact it was a collection of the amusing blunders about nature which we have seen in older writers with hundreds of such bits of ancient wisdom as:

"The bite of the cockatrice is death to the weasel unless that animal has eaten some rue.

"When a crocodile sees a man it weeps over him [hence "crocodile tears"] and then devours him."

There is a long description of dragons, which were then (and for centuries later) as real to men as domestic cats. They are said to be perpetually at feud with elephants and have other quaint ways:

"Often four or five of them tie their tails together, rear up their heads, and fly over the sea in search of good food."

Large numbers of books about animals, or "Bestiaries," on these lines circulated in the homes of the new middle class, and they hardly went beyond the natural history of Aristotle. Besides the dragon various other fabulous beasts, such as the unicorn, the basilisk, and the griffin were implicitly believed to exist in foreign parts. In fact one story ran that a basilisk strayed into the city of Rome and several people who caught its eye fell down dead. The theologians, who had to admit that God put this fatal eye in the basilisk, added that he compelled the animal to give a loud cry to warn mortals not to look at it whenever it left its den. Animals that are well known were described with touches of wisdom from 1,000 or 2,000 years before. "The eagle" said the learned cleric Gerald of Cambrai, "lives so long that its life rivals eternity itself. It flies so high that the sun often scorches its wings." The spontaneous generation of marine animals, insects, etc., continued to be an article of faith until centuries later. The earthly origin and prophetic nature of comets also were universally believed. When one appeared in 1456 Pope Calixtus III, who was supposed to be learned, ordered "several days prayer to avert the wrath of God or, if a calamity impended, turn it against the Turks rather than the Christians." The contemporary

27

Vatican archivist Platina says that the Pope excommunicated the comet. Others now discovered that the howling of a dog at night or the tick of the "death-watch" beetle portended death. One learned writer discovered that a safe way of prolonging life was to suck in the breath of a girl or young woman. It was widely discussed, and it is on record that a distinguished but aged physician retired from practice and rented rooms in a boarding school for girls.

Medicine, the one branch of "science" that was honored, was still inconceivably crude. The circulation of the blood was entirely unknown, and the promising fund of chemical discovery that the Arabs had made was so far neglected that the pharmacopeia was almost as bad as in ancient Egypt. The devil was still made responsible for disease, particularly of the brain or if the patient had had nightmares, and the most noxious or filthy substances, often human excrements, were used to drive him out. Here are a few recipes:

"For nocturnal visitations of devils make a salve of these 12 herbs [calculated to give a savage a nightmare] . . . Put them under the altar, boil them in butter and sheep's grease, add a lot of blessed salt and strain through a cloth.

"When a devil possesses a man and controls him from within by disease a spew-drink of lupin, bishops wort, henbane, and garlic should be given. Pound them together and add holy water.

"A drink for a fiend-sick man, to be drunk out of the church bell: giltripe, avaglossum, yarrow, lupin, flower-de-luce, fennel, lichen, and losage. Work up to a drink with clear ale, sing seven masses over it, and add garlic and holy water."

There was an infinite variety of drugs—note how the profit of the clergy comes in—and nearly all of them had no more relation to the disease than to the weather. Some dispensed with drugs and simply went for the devil who caused the disease. The patient was grievously manhandled or compelled to swallow his excrements. He was abused in terms which, we are told, must not be translated today. Others hurled at the devil big Greek or other words taken from the black magic or occultism of the time or even the early Christian controversies: Tetragrammaton, Homoousion, Acheron, etc. It is piquant to imagine doctors or priests howling this rubbish at a chained lunatic 2,000 years after Aristotle. Travel greatly enriched the pharmacopeia or the profit of the druggist. Ground-up coral or dried blood of rats, bats, toads, or criminals, fibers of the hangman's rope, dried menstrual blood of a virgin—all these were on sale in Paris even in the golden age of Louis XIV in the 17th century. A dentist was known as a "tooth-breaker." The barber was the surgeon, clapping mud or hot pitch over the stump when he amputated a leg. We begin to wonder why the average expectation of life was even as much as 30 years or so. As to the amiable writers who persuade you that these folk had a jolly and virtuous time in the Middle Ages . . .

At one time a genius arose who discovered that God had really given indications which of the herbs and roots in nature were efficacious for this or that ailment. Blood-wood was clearly intended for the purification of the blood. Plants with yellow flowers must be intended to cure jaundice. Walnuts, with their curious resemblance to the cerebral hemispheres when the skull is removed, are the predestined cure for diseases of the brain. Liverwort, the leaves of which vaguely recall the liver in shape, are meant to cure that organ. Eyebright, which has bright spots like eyes on the leaves, is the remedy for eye-diseases. Red flannel is bound to be good for rheumatism since it has the color of blood.

At last the era of scientific drugs or "medical chemistry" arrived. The man who was chiefly instrumental in introducing it, Paracelsus, impressed his own age as the greatest master of these centuries—apart from art—and, while his record is so puzzling that modern historians of chemistry give us different estimates of him, he does seem to have had exceptional ability; though, Sir Edward Thorpe says, he "squandered his powers in dissipation." It is curious that the same thing is said of one of the greatest physicians of the Arab-Persian world, Ibn-Sina. If it is true that, as Thorpe says, "during the greater part of his waking time he was more or less intoxicated," he must have been head and shoulders above his age to make such a mark on it. Experts doubt if he wrote any of the books which circulated under his name, so I will not quote from them but take a few general statements about him from Thorpe.

He was a master of the chemistry of his time and knew every element and compound that the Arabs had added to the final chemistry of the Greeks. His chief merit was that he tried to correct the degeneration of chemistry into alchemy and insisted that the proper use of it was to provide drugs for the remedy of disease. I have said that practically every prince and bishop had an alchemist to turn base metals into gold for him and discover the elixir of life or the draught that would give him perpetual youth. Thorpe shows that it was in fact in this period, not in the Arab world, that this gross perversion of science took place. "The philosopher's stone is first heard of in the 12th century," he says, and "the universal medicine and the elixir of life were the products of a later age." Professors who, to please the orthodox, say that it was the Arabs who diverted chemistry into this monstrous field of fraud and folly do not know the history of the science. This period, Thorpe says, "produced an abundant literature, mainly the work of ecclesiastics," but it is simply "a long chapter in the history of human credulity . . . for the most part a record of self-deception, imposture, and fraud." Of seven leading names he gives five are the names of friars and one of a canon. Yet the three products that these writers professed to supply—the chemicals for turning stuff into gold, curing all diseases, and prolonging life—may, with astrology, almost be said to have obsessed the minds of the rich and noble during these four centuries. Thorpe gives a string of names of princes, generals, nobles, and prelates who had their alchemists.

Paracelsus opposed this. But he was himself an impudent character of "boundless effrontery." He was a dipsomaniac and a mystic, a fierce critic of medical traditions and an astrologer. Of the pupils and followers of the critic who probably wrote the works that bear his name Thorpe says:

"They were all zealous anti-Galenists, who professed to believe that the sum and perfection of human knowledge was to be found in the Cabala, and that the secrets of magical medicine were contained in the Apocalypse. They adopted pantheism in all its grossness; everything that exists eats, drinks, and voids excrement; even minerals and liquids assimilate food and eliminate what they do not incorporate; Sylphs inhabit the air, nymphs the water, pigmies the earth, and salamanders the fire. The laws of the Cabala were held to explain the functions of the body. The sun rules the heart, the moon the brain (hence 'lunatics'), Jupiter the liver, Saturn the spleen, Mercury the lungs, Mars the bile, Venus the kidneys. Gold was a specific against diseases of the heart; the liquor of Luna (solution of silver) cures diseases of the brain. 'The remedies,' said Paracelsus, 'are subjected to the will of the stars and directed by them. You ought, therefore, to wait until heaven is favorable before ordering a medicine.' "

Apart from art, as I have said, this man was the most influential thinker of the most brilliant period of medieval Rome: the time when, we are told, the invention of printing and the discovery of America had greatly enlarged the mind of Europe. Modern authorities are, as Hillier says in his "History of Medicine," not agreed whether he was a charlatan or a man of "brilliant intellect." His chief strength was that there was the beginning of a revolt against mere authority—against the slavery to Galen in medicine, to Aristotle in philosophy, and to the Papacy in religion—and he took the lead. He had, or tried to get, a philosophical, you might almost say a scientific conception of the relation of man to the universe and, he felt sure that the world which caused disease also provided remedies. It was "dissatisfaction with Aristotle, who ruled the universities in this respect that drove him to the mystic and occultists."

There has been such a determined and unscrupulous effort in America in recent years to persuade people that at least by the 16th century—1,300 years after the conversion of Constantine—Christian Europe had become learned, and the great art of the Roman school is so well known that some readers may wonder if I have not selected as representatives of the age men whose opinions it is easy to ridicule. Read for yourself the article on the period (Renaissance) in the Encyclopedia Americana, which, to the discredit of its editors, is written by a Jesuit who chiefly wanted to do the best he could for his church. The only other "great" men, besides artists, whom he names are Valla (an erotic poet and historian who was driven into hypocritical subservience by the Popes), Cardinal Nicholas of Cusa (a good mathematician muzzled by high ecclesiastical honors), and a few classical scholars or Platonist philosophers. A Protestant would add Wyclif and John Hus, but their work is purely theological. Other men whose names are familiar—Gutenberg and Columbus—were neither great men nor writers. But there is, leaving pioneers of science to a later chapter, one other whose opinions it is interesting to notice.

Bayle Calls Cardano, a contemporary of Paracelsus and like him a master of medicine, "one of the greatest geniuses of his age." He was also one of the most eccentric men of his age, a fanatic for astrology, a desperate gambler, a professor of immeasurable conceit who considered himself the redeemer of the world; and he thus naively described himself in his autobiography, which we have.

In his frequent fits of depression he bit his arms and laid a whip on his buttocks; which does not seem to have been for the usual purpose as he says that he was moderate with women because the sex-act "upset my stomach." He was impotent from the age of 21 to the age of 31 because, he says, he was born under an unfavorable conjunction of the planets. He claimed the power of second sight and of passing into an ecstasy whenever he wished. "It begins," he says, "in my head, principally the cerebellum, and goes down the spine of my back." He claimed to have a guiding spirit and to be able to forecast events by marks on his nails. He wrote most extensively on astrology, with hundreds of such decisions as these:

"The Moon with the Dragon's Tail in a Nativity gives suspicion of the mother's honesty and hints that the child is not of the reputed father's begetting.

"The Moon in Aquarius or Pisces makes the Native disliked by Princes, Grandees, and the Upper Ten [somebody has here pencilled in the copy I am reading that this was the horoscope of Goethe.]

"A primary cause of men leading single lives is the combination of the Moon with Saturn in their nativity."

He was a strong believer in the influence of the mother on the child she bore; for instance, if she ate plenty of crabs while bearing, the child would like crabs. In medicine, of which he was one of the leading professors, he taught such absurdities as that to cure brain-disease you must anoint the coronal suture with a mixture of tar and honey, and he orders a diet of turtle soup, snails, barley water, and asses' milk. But the treatment of disease was still, in the middle of the century, so crude that I could fill a book with absurdities. As to the work in which Cardano explained nature to his generation, it would provide another volume of absurdities.

I said from the first that while we find a pardonable amusement in the ancient errors, since each of these men helped or tried to help the growth of knowledge and it is no merit of ours that we are wiser, we begin to have other feelings as we approach modern times. After the fine beginning of real wisdom that was made by the Ionians, Epicureans, and Alexandrians, and the further development of science and history by Arabs and Persians, we have a right to expect something better than this 2,000 years after Thales, Buddha, and Confucius. We know why we do not get it. The pace of science is necessarily much slower in its earlier stages when it has not yet developed even a moderate technique, but the Arabs, if not the Alexandrians, had begun this. It was the principles solidly established by Aquinas for the church that had arrested progress. And the stagnant and odoriferous state of the stream of knowledge was not only in regard to the interpretation of nature and man. The development of the code of conduct was just as backward, although it had reached almost its modern stage in the Maxims of Ptah-Hotep 3,000 years earlier. Law was barbarous in comparison with the Hammurabi Code of 3,000 years earlier. It was the age of the Spanish Inquisition, of savage religious wars, of the beginning of black slavery, of the sordid exploitation of four-fifths of the race, of a 90 percent illiteracy in most countries, of the subjection of women. It was the last hour of the monopoly of power by the Roman Church; and it was, on the church's own code, the most immoral period in the history of Europe.

V. LUTHER AND THE REFORMERS

The Reformation introduces a different type of absurdity and one that we do not so easily forgive. At the time when Luther diverted half of Europe from the mumbling of Masses and the windy speculations of the medieval Schoolmen to the reading of the Bible science was beginning to make progress. Anyone who knows to what height the Arabs and Persians had carried the science of the Alexandrians finds the progress appallingly slow. The Alexandrian Greeks and the Spanish Arabs had made more progress in two centuries than medieval Christendom, for all its Renaissance, made in five, though the world now had the technique and instruments that the Arabs had developed.

The Scholastic theologians, the Popes and the Aristotelic philosophers had checked the study of science, to the profound loss of the race. Astronomy and other branches of science were now advancing, and, as Huxley would put it 350 years later, they came up against the notice: "No Road—By order, Moses." From this time onward we get a series of blunders and absurdities, even from the pens of men of superior intellect, which we do not regard with the leniency with which we have smiled at errors in the preceding chapters. In the name of religion men not only frown upon the new way of attaining truth but they deny such truths as are attained and burn men at the stake (Giordano Bruno) or hand them over to the Inquisition (Galileo) for stating them. Protestantism, in its first phase being essentially a biblical religion, sinned heavily in this respect, though it was in Protestant lands that science was presently to make the greatest progress.

We will not search too closely the works of the skeptical Humanists, like Erasmus, who "laid the egg that Luther hatched." They were literary men—they took their name at that time from their "humane" or profane as distinct from sacred studies—and had no interest in the scrutiny of nature. Indeed it was by such works as his "Praise of Folly" and "Colloquies" that Erasmus best served the world, and one finds little to quarrel with in those entertaining works. He is, in fact, not consistent. He seems to endorse original sin and the immaculate conception of Mary when, in his commentary on the gospel of Luke, he says: "Where there is lust the fruit is unclean." This is not only out of character but he elsewhere plainly rejects the idea of original sin. No man really knows the extent of his skepticism or his religion. "It is not everybody who has the stuff of martyrs," he says, "and I believe that if trouble befel me I would imitate St. Peter." He decided to pass through life along a comfortable path and would not join the German Reformers, alleging that he did not like revolts against authority. In any case a search for absurdities in the works of Erasmus would be so unprofitable that I have not given any time to it.

Head and front of all the Reformers, idol and saint of the Protestant branch of the Christian Church, is Martin Luther, the ex-monk who first openly raised the banner of revolt against the Papacy and, aided by political conditions in Germany, did effectively found Protestantism. Since he did not profess to have any other learning than theological, and theological stupidities are sufficiently familiar in our own time to be ignored here, it may seem that there can be little in his writings to interest us; especially as he was a typical case of "glandular personality" and his crude language is apt to be just an expression of his vigorous hormones. But, as Protestants chose to thrust aside the more refined, or less boorish, Melanchthon and Zwingli and accept Luther as the figure-head of their purified version of Christianity, and they write and talk as much nonsense about him as Catholics do about Aquinas, it is worth while to devote a page to his blunders. The chief interest is that while the Reformation, in bringing the world back to the teaching of Jesus in the New Testament, is supposed to shine in him with much light and mystic favor in comparison with the sensuality of the Roman Church in Renaissance days, it is mainly Luther's moral and social crudities, vulgarity, and gross taste that offend us.

The controversy over the man was so fierce at the time and the controversialists on both sides, however pious, were so unscrupulous and indelicate that it is not easy sometimes to find the truth. A well-known Catholic writer of the time, Cajetanus, says in one of his poems that Luther was the offspring of an "incubus," or male devil, and many other of his colleagues said that he came straight from hell to poison the virtuous world—the world I described in the preceding chapter! The more "scientific" Catholics consulted the astrologers, who were as numerous and prosperous as psychiatrists are today. Unfortunately the day and hour of Luther's birth were disputed, but this did not restrain them from pronouncing such verdicts as this:

"It appears from his horoscope that the combination of planets made him a most bitter and most profane enemy of the Christian faith . . . He died without a sense of religion and his soul, steeped in guilt, sailed to hell, there to be lashed to death by the fiery whips of Alecto, Tisiphon, and Megaera (the Greek Furies) through endless ages."

We simple-minded moderns wonder why he was so punished if the planets had inexorably made him a heretic, and how a spiritual soul is whipped on its ethereal buttocks, but it is useless to look for common sense or common fairness in matters of religion. It was then common to ascribe the Reformation to the stars, but it is almost as bad of the modern Catholic writer to attribute it to "lust" when we see that the Catholic world of the time put no bridle at all on lust. But with these Catholic pleasantries we could fill a long chapter. Bishop Bossuet says that in a sermon on Christian marriage Luther, advising men who found their wives churlish in bed, said: "If the mistress will not give in, call the maid"; and that there were not five virgins over the age of 20 in any city and he did not blame the girls. Even modern Jesuits contend in their lives of Luther that he had syphilis.

I have elsewhere shown that the truth is between these Catholic libels and the Protestant eulogies. Luther commonly, in his mature years, used language which would make a modern preacher even of liberal ways blush to the roots of his hair. If you happen to have read a rare pamphlet (circulated privately) by Mark Twain giving an imaginary conversation at the court of Queen Elizabeth, you get near it. It was not far short of that or of Rabelais' language. The interest of it is that it was the custom of his age, lingering from the Middle Ages. The Pope virtually excused Rabelais from his vows for his skill in that sort of thing, although he knew that the chief professed aim of the French writer was to blunt the edge of Catholic hostility to the Protestants which it was the duty of every good Catholic to sharpen. Here I am concerned only with blunders and absurdities. You find them numerous enough in his *Table Talk*:

"Before Noah's flood the world was highly learned because men lived a long time and so attained great experience and wisdom. Now before we begin rightly to come to a true knowledge of a thing we are let down and die. God will not have that we should attain a higher knowledge of things (C L X, Hazlitt's translation)."

It seems from the note on this in Bayle's Dictionary that there was in the later Middle Ages a large literature about the immense learning of Adam and the patriarchs. Aristotle was a schoolboy in comparison with Adam; and he was as handsome as he was wise. Some of the medieval rabbis, and even the learned Maimonides, believed that Adam was a hermaphrodite, and that when the drama of life on earth is over the two sexes will again be blended in each individual. It seems more promising even than the Mohammedan paradise. Luther again says:

"Adam had more children than the three that are mentioned in the Bible . . . a full 200, I am persuaded. For he lived to a great, great age—930 years. Adam and Eve entered the garden about noon and, having appetites to eat, she took the apple; thus the Fall was about 2 of the clock according to the account." (D L VIII.)

"Neither Cicera nor Vergil nor Demosthenes is to be compared with David in point of eloquence." (D L XI.)

"When the devil intends to hurt us the loving holy angels drive him away, for the angels have long arms . . . No malady comes to us from God. They all come from the devil . . . I should have no compassion on witches. I would burn all of them . . . The Emperor Frederic invited a necromancer to dine with him and by his knowledge of magic turned his guests into griffins."

"The whole firmament moves swiftly round . . . and this is doubtless done by an angel . . . If the sun and stars were composed of iron, steel, silver, or gold they would melt."

"There is no gown or garment that worse becomes a woman than the desire to be wise."

"It is certain that swans sing very melodiously at their death."

He professed to be as familiar with the devil as a man is with his dog, and in his work "On Private Masses" gives a long account of him and his conversations with him.

"The devil knows how to urge and apply his arguments with great force. He has a strong, deep voice, and the disputes are not transacted in long or many meditations, but in a moment the question and the answer are dispatched. I know that from this course some have been found dead in their beds at break of day. For he is able to squeeze and strangle the body, and not this only, for in these disputes he can press the soul and reduce it to such straits as in a moment to drive it out, to which extremity he has more than once reduced me. I verily believe that Emserus and Oecolampadius and other such men, struck by these fiery darts and javelins of Satan, have perished by a sudden death . . . I know the devil intimately, having eaten more than one bushel of salt with him. The devil much oftener sleeps with me, and lies nearer to me, than my Catherine. He used to walk with me in my bedroom. I have had him hang about my neck." (Quoted from Bayle.)

Such was, according to some 100,000,000 educated folk in modern civilizations, the greatest man between St. Paul and Napoleon. I leave it to them to puzzle out his wide departure from the asceticism of the Bible which he imposed upon Europe, for in his mature years he glorified "the flesh" and enjoyed it so much that he saw no other use in women and called them by names that I may not repeat. But his aberrations in regard to social questions are more relevant. He despised the workers as much as he despised clever women, philosophers, or scientists. A Protestant theologian, Dr. Betcke, has a work with the title "Luther's Social Ethic," and the learned contents may be summed up in the phrase that Luther had no social ethic. He found none in his New Testament. When the German workers, the peasants particularly, claimed that they were entitled to the justice of which the Bible spoke, Luther in two famous letters told the princes and landowners to "shoot them down like mad dogs." Betcke quotes him saying:

"As to the common people, Mr. Everybody, one has to be hard with them and see that they do their work and that under the threat of the sword and the law they comply with the observances of piety; just as you chain up wild beasts so as to get a peaceful life. Secular authority has to see to it that God is honored and feared."

He owed the success of the Reformation to the princes, who, since their emperor at that time was a foreigner, were comparatively easily induced to rebel. But it is worth noting that Luther excused himself from taking any interest in social or political reform on the ground that the New Testament did not direct him to do so.

The errors in natural history or physiology of which I have given so many specimens are amusing but intelligible. The age of real scientific method had not yet arrived. But so many folk insist that the science had been enriched and irradiated by the Christian religion that the moral blunders of Augustine, Aquinas, and Luther have a more important place in any collection of absurdities. And if this was the mind of Luther we will not linger over the other Reformers. The sour asceticism, in fact savagery—when we think of the burning of a good man like Servetus for denying the myth of the Trinity—of Calvin I decline to discuss, and the writings of the more liberal and more accomplished Zwingli and Melanchthon are almost entirely theological. One absurdity that was common to the Reformers and directly due to their bibliolatry was that they persisted in the old idea of the earth being the center of the universe. Luther had said in reference to the Copernican theory:

"People give ear to an upstart astrologer who tried to show that the earth revolves, not the heavens or the firmament, the sun and the moon. Whoever wishes to appear clever must devise some new system . . . This fool (Copernicus) wishes to reverse the entire science of astronomy, but Holy Scripture tells us that Joshua commanded the sun, not the earth, to stand still . . . We know on the authority of Moses that longer ago than 6,000 years this world did not exist."

We are not surprised to find the hard-boiled Calvin asking:

"Who will venture to place the authority of Copernicus above that of the Holy Scriptures?"

But even Melanchthon, who is counted the most liberal and cultivated of the Reformers, wrote:

"The eyes are witnesses that the heavens revolve in the space of 24 hours. But certain men, either from the love of novelty or to make a display of ingenuity, have concluded that the earth moves . . . It is a lack of honesty and decency to assert such ideas."

He fixes the date of creation at 3963 B.C. and, of course, incidentally echoes all the blunders about nature that, as we saw, have come down from the age of Aristotle. What is worse, he emphatically endorses such mischievous superstitions as astrology, witchcraft, diabolical possession, and all practices and gossip connected with them. Dr. Hartfelds has given us a special essay on "The Superstition of Philip Melanchthon" and given ample evidence on these points.

In a "Declamation on the Dignity of Astrology" he sets out to prove that its teaching is not only true but beneficial to the human race. He says:

"I not only find usefulness in the art, as I perceive in medicine and other matters, but it is more important that when I behold this marvellous correspondence of the heavenly bodies with things here below, the order and harmony remind me that the world is not due to chance but ruled by divinity . . . I do not think that any man is so superstitious that he will deny that the observation of the stars helps the physician."

With the devil he is almost as familiar as Luther, though he does not claim as much personal experience. Dreams, to which he paid the most serious attention, constantly describing his dreams to his friends, are often due to the devil. They are of four classes: natural, prognostic of future events, divine, and diabolical. In somnambulism it is the devil who is active.

"Satan leads sleeping persons out of their bedroom to steep and dangerous places, and if the angels do not guard them they are killed."

He accepts stories of such things and of possession and black magic with extraordinary credulity, but I need not reproduce them. "God," he says, "has given the devil and the sorcerer power over men." He knows one of these sorcerers whom the devil took on his back and flew up to an immense height. And so on. It would be tiresome to reproduce his stories.

If this was, under biblical influence, the frame of mind of the most cultivated of the Reformers we need not consider any of the others. I pass on rather to certain opinions of the early Jesuits though they did not appear until later in the century. Life was too strenuous for them to notice the tears of the crocodile or the immodest habits of the beaver, the solidity of the firmament and revolutions of the sun, and frivolities of that nature. On the other hand their profound discoveries in philosophy and theology interest no man today outside the stuffy atmosphere of a Catholic university. What calls for a word is the claim, now repeated on all sides in America, that those great early theologians, Cardinal Bellarmine and Father Suarez, gave the world, and the fathers of the American Revolution, the ideas of freedom and democracy.

The reader will get an amusing light on this claim if he will examine Catholic American literature in its chonological order. Forty years ago Catholics put their world-scholarship into a most expensive Catholic Encyclopedia. It, of course, has an orthodox article on Suarez, the supposed inspirer of modern democracy, and *it does not make any claim whatever that he did this.* It gives 13 points as characteristic of his thought. They are such things as "the principle of individuation by the proper concrete entity of beings," "the pure potentiality of matter," "the singular as the object of direct intellectual cognition," and so on. I doubt if the modern world would take the trouble to think out whether these things are absurd or not. Thirty years later appeared that generally admirable work, The Encyclopedia of the Social Sciences, with an article on Suarez by a Catholic professor, and he says that in his Defense of the Catholic Faith the Jesuit lays down that the authority of a government "depends upon the consent of the governed" and that sovereignty is "given by God to the people."

He is candid enough to remind the reader that this work of the Jesuit is a reply to a work in which the English King James I defended the divine right of Kings; and that gives you the correct slant on the whole business. When, in the 14th century, Marsiglio of Padua, one of the most learned of the Italians, argued for "the sovereignty of the people" or the replacing of the royal authority of the Popes in Italy by a republic, he was a heretic and an outcast. But a number of the kings of Europe were now Protestants, and the Jesuits were conspiring everywhere to get rid of them. So they now discover that a King does not hold power by a divine commission but from the people or by "natural right," so the people—in the case of Protestant kings—have every right to get rid of them. It was part of the Jesuit conspiracy against Protestant powers. The Vatican recognized it as such and continued to the second half of the 19th century to encourage Catholic kings to assert that they ruled by divine right and to rebuke the removal of kings, as at the French Revolution, as sacrilege.

The whole thing is, in fact, a typical scholastic juggling with words, and the suggestion that men like Jefferson were influenced by it is ludicrous. According to Catholic theology, then and now, "divine right" (or law) is of two kinds: natural and positive. The amoral law (apart from the Bible) is, for instance, "natural," but since God is the author of Nature it is also divine. If you read German you can follow the whole rigmarole of Suarez's argument in Dr. H. Bommer's "Staatslehre des Franz Suarez." It starts from Adam and his progeny. When his descendants became numerous enough to form communities the "mystic political body" appointed its authorities. Even Catholics had never suggested that in ancient or pagan times Kings ruled by divine right, and the Jesuit craftily avoids noticing that in Christian times it was supposed to be the consecration by the church that made a king's person sacred. His argument compels him to say that "all men are born free" but don't imagine for a moment that the American and French Revolutions borrowed this phrase from the Jesuit. It would follow that he must condemn slavery, and this he refused to do. Men are born equal in nature as God created it, but—here he expressly refers to and follows St. Augustine—the sins of men perverted it and slavery is "a consequence of sin" (as Augustine does say in his "City of God").

As to that other and brighter ornament of early Jesuitry, Cardinal Bellarmine—in getting authorization for the Society the founder had sworn that members would never accept dignities—the man who engineered the first condemnation of Galileo, he trimmed like—well, like a Jesuit. He did talk like Suarez about the sovereignty (under God) of the people, but when the Jesuits who in England conspired against Elizabeth appealed to his authority he disowned it. He wrote:

"Disobedience to rulers, is a far worse sin than the abuse of powers on the part of the ruler."

He maintained—so did Suarez—all the principles on which Catholic intolerance is based. A king is bound to protect religion, and, as there is only one true religion, he is bound to suppress all attacks on it:

"Civil authorities must lend their arm to the church to suppress heretical writings and punish obstinate heretics."

There must be no toleration of non-Catholics in a Catholic state, for "freedom of religion leads to the ruin of the people," but Protestant kings must not persecute Catholics, and Catholic kings are bound to fight heretical kings (as the King of Spain was driven against England). Both his writings and those of Suarez are full of the moral monstrosities to which the teaching of Aquinas leads, and the recent "discovery" that the leaders of the American Revolution were inspired by them is on a par with the discovery that King Solomon of Judea knew all about uranium and atomic energy.

VI. PIONEERS OF THE MODERN AGE

In spite of this heavier theological tyranny of the 16th century modern thought was stirring in the womb of Europe. Historians generally say that what they call Modern Times began in the middle of the 16th century but there is little ground for saying it. In fact, when we remember that the development of printing, the spirited exploration of the globe, the Reformation, and the Copernican discovery occurred in the preceding century (1450-1550) and no great innovations like these occurred between 1550 and 1750 the division of chronological periods seems absurd. You might say that there was the brilliant flowering of the Elizabethan Age. Not only, however, was this almost purely literary, but it was almost confined to one century. A lamentable decay began in Spain and Italy, France and Germany were almost paralyzed by the ferocious wars of Catholic and Protestant, and promising civilizations like that of Bohemia were ruined. Hence, passing over the great poets, dramatists, and artists generally, to whom we do not look for intellectual absurdities, there were not many great men of interest to examine from our present angle.

JEAN BODIN

It is interesting to consider first the writings of one of the ablest men of the 16th century, the great French lawyer Jean Bodin (1530-96). Probably few American readers today will recognize the name, but the French count him not only the ablest jurist of the age but "the founder of the philosophy of history," the best economist of his time, the most distinguished political theorist, and the most learned man. Since he was in his age repeatedly denounced for skepticism, J. M. Robertson is eager to include him in his "History of Freethought," but is neither clear nor consistent. He agrees that Bodin was "one of the most powerful minds of the age" and wrote "one of the most powerful treatises on government between Aristotle and our own age," but to say on one page that "his Rationalism on some heads is beyond doubt" and on the next that he was "a believing Catholic" is peculiar. And when Robertson says that he wrote "an original outline of a naturalist philosophy" he shows that he never read it. For this "Amphitheater of Nature," or "Account of the Efficient and Final Causes of All Things," presents Bodin to us as a figure of remarkable mental stature on the brink between the medieval world and the new but, as far as positive knowledge is concerned, belonging entirely to the Middle Ages.

As the book is cast in a scientific form it begins with a long description of the universe and the creation of it. The universe is, of course, the toy theater of the earlier Greeks with the earth at its center. He contemptuously rejects the Copernican theory and describes the earth and the various heavens above it on the lines which I have already described. Where he is original he is generally more absurd than his predecessors. Thus:

> "The opinion of Democritus leads me to think that comets are the souls of illustrious men who, having been on the earth for an infinite number of years, are in the end reduced to the common extremity of all things that are born and have an end. Hence one of two things must be true: either this is the final triumph of their blessed lives or they return to the starry heavens as luminous orbs. Hence also, I think, the fact that famines, pestilences, and wars then occur, as if the cities and their people were abandoned by their governors and good captains, who had been accustomed to appease the fury of the divine majesty by their presence."

He then proceeds in scientific fashion to divide terrestrial things into minerals, plants, and animals. He says:

> "There are six metals—gold, silver, brass, tin, lead, and iron, as is stated in the Scriptures. More than these will never be found . . . Quicksilver is an invention of chemists who made it in order to bring up the number of metals to the number of the planets.
> "Between minerals and plants we have Silver Tree, which is found growing in mines."

He means the branching veins of silver in the rock, which he thinks grew there, and assures the reader that some have been known to grow to a height of 60 feet. There are organisms also between the plant and animal worlds.

> "The coral is something between plants and animals. It dif-

fers from the Silver Tree in the fact that it derives its nourishment from its roots and produces branches covered with bark and moss, while the Silver Tree has no conspicuous roots . . .

"The Iogue (the sensitive mimosa, recently discovered in the West Indies) of the Indies is . . . something we have heard of from the Spaniards, but it is a fact it is not a plant but a Zoophyte.

"A Zoophyte has the nature of both plant and animal. Such are mother-of-pearl, sponges, and oysters.

"It would be rash to assert that the sponge is formed from the foam of the sea because another sponge grows when you tear one away.

"Many have thought that in certain parts of Scotland the trees bear apples which fall into the water and grow into geese, but the inhabitants have carefully observed, and they seem to think that what happens is that the trees bear cockles, as the rocks in the sea do, and that when these fill up and grow to their full stature they open and let out little birds that swim about in the water."

There are hundreds of these entertaining bits of natural history but I have already given plenty of specimens. It is all derived from that stream of traditional error that flows on from early Greek times, and our only serious thought about it is to reflect that if the scientific methods of the Alexandrian Greeks, further improved by the Arabs, had been adopted in Christendom we should not have the spectacle of a great mind of the 16th century hoarding such absurdities. But the next book of Bodin's that I choose, "The Demoniomaniacs" (in the French version "The Plague of Demons") shows how this great mind was too steeped in the superstitions of the Middle Ages to turn, as Bacon would presently do, to the direct and critical study of nature. However sincerely Bodin pleaded for religious toleration, as any scholarly statesmen of that bloodily fanatical age might be expected to do, the deepest-rooted belief in his mind was in the Catholic teaching about the devils, and if he was so profoundly convinced on that point it is useless to suppose that he rejected any doctrines.

It was the age of witchcraft, a time when, one historian estimates, several million men, women, and even children were burned alive in four centuries for worshipping the devil. I have shown in one of my Little Blue Books that there was in fact an organized cult of Satan (or the Spirit), a revulsion against the sexual hypocrisy of Christendom and a frank cultivation of sensuality. But, although the German theologian Wier had already started a revolt against the persecution, Bodin took up the blindly medieval position and showed, for a great lawyer, an amazing credulity. The single point on which any serious person can raise any suspicion of skepticism in his case is that in the fanatical and increasing hostility of Catholic and Protestant he pleaded for toleration. That might well be explained by his position as a statesman. The ferocious struggle was retarding the progress of France and threatened to ruin a large part of Europe, as it presently did.

However that may be, in this book Bodin shows a fierce belief in one of the crudest superstitions of Christianity. Even in his introductory remarks he gives amusing absurdities. Aristotle's view of the origin of springs is entirely wrong when he says that "the water comes from putrefaction in underground caverns":

"The Hebrew philosophers and even Solomon have shown that they come from the sea just as the veins of the human body start from the liver."

Again, it is notoriously false that, as Aristotle held, "the rainbow is never seen at night." The Schoolman Albert the Great has proved that this is wrong, he says. Aristotle is not only wrong in affirming that the material universe is eternal but "he is the only one of the Greek philosophers to allege this . . . even the Epicureans laughed at him for saying it." As if any Greek philosopher, least of all an Epicurean, thought that matter had been created! But even Aristotle is brought in as a witness to the reality of witchcraft:

"He writes that in one of the seven Isles of Aeolus (out on the Atlantic) a marvellous sound of trumpets, drums, and cymbals is heard. These are the meetings and dances of the witches."

They travel vast distances—in one place he represents them as flying on broomsticks—in a few seconds, as is proved by a crowd of witnesses from ancient and Christian times. In every chapter he speaks of the *incubi and succubi*—devils which "lie on" (a woman) and devils which, in female form, "lie under"—and tells how they have a preference for animal bodies:

"It is a curious thing that Satan, who is accustomed to assume any sort of body he likes, most frequently, in fact usually, takes the form of a goat; that is to say, of a filthy and stinking animal. That is why in Holy Scripture the devils are called goats.

"We read of a male witch of Berne named Stasus who had many enemies, and he often suddenly disappeared from the midst of them and could be killed only when he was asleep. He left two disciples, and these men could cause tempests and hurricanes."

He believes as firmly in the superstition of the were-wolf as in the existence of cats and dogs and piles up pages of evidence:

"We have a case that was tried and published in France . . . A male witch named Gernier on the Feast of St. Matthew, being in the form of a were-wolf, seized a girl of 10 or 12 years in a vineyard and killed her with his claws and teeth, ate her legs and arms, and took some of the body to his wife. He tried to do the same a fortnight later but was prevented by three men, and he was burned alive. There are many other cases."

Of the witch-meetings, which were real enough, he has the usual fantastic ideas:

"Some danced by the light of candles of green wax and made sacrifices to the devil. Then they anointed themselves and were turned into wolves which ran with incredible speed, then they returned to human form and back into wolves again . . . They killed young children and ate them . . . they killed many people by sprinkling a powder on them."

Later he devotes many pages of what he calls judicially-authenticated cases of copulation with devils; though "the seed was cold," he says. There are thousands of known cases, he affirms; in fact "an infinite number" of cases. One is of a Spanish abbess who confessed that she had had intercourse with a devil for 30 years, ever since her 13th year. Love-letters from the devil were produced in court, and so on.

I have dwelt a little longer than usual on this writer, partly because he was one of the ablest and most learned writers of Europe in his century but chiefly because *this was the common frame of mind and set of beliefs of even the most educated men and women only three or four centuries ago.* All those learned Jesuits who were so "modern" had the same ideas. These are therefore not merely pleasant reading, as we have found them in earlier times, but instructive. That such things should survive more than 1,000 years after the Alexandrian Epicureans had taught men to observe critically and think for themselves was due to the hostility to science and the opposition of the church when Europe was reawakened.

MONTAIGNE

But the growth of wealth and the advance of culture had created a large lay middle class, and a few of these men began to think. Best known of them today is Montaigne (1533-92), the famous French essayist, who was exactly contemporary with Bodin. The word "essay" is rather misleading to us. Montaigne was the first to use it, and it was part of his plan to conceal his few vague heresies in a discursive collection of reflections on innocent matters. That he was a skeptic is as unquestionable as the fact that in such an age he would have been burned, as others were, if he had said so in plain French. "He lived," says the French Encyclopedia, "in the most frightful epoch of our history"; and the sole cause of the frightfulness was religious passion, for the Italian Renaissance had already spread to France and England and was restoring civilization. The change of religion was then costing Europe as heavy a price as the change of economic system is costing in our time, and it was a particularly bad time to profess disbelief in both religions.

But the inquirer after absurdities finds a monumental difference between the skeptic Montaigne and the believing Bodin or the theologians. His writing is almost always sane, wise, and humane. As a purely literary man—apart, of course, from his work as a great lawyer he knows no more about science than literary men do today, and he rejects the Copernican system. Of the dispute of the two astronomical theories he says:

"What shall we reap by it but only that we need not care which of the two systems it be? Who knoweth whether a hundred years hence a third person will arise who happily shall overthrow his two predecessors?"

He is blamed by astronomers also for a foolish criticism of the recent reform of the calendar. On the other hand he rejected the belief in witchcraft, though discreetly. In the essay "On Miracles and Witchcraft" he says, ironically:

"The witches of my neighborhood go in peril of their lives at the instance of every new author who arrives to give body to their fantasies."

What follows is an abstract discussion of the fallibility of evidence, but in the end he tells how a prince whom he visited took him—"to put an end to my incredulity," he says—to see a witch, an old hag of the proverbial type. He even saw her witch-mark. He ends vaguely but says that he would "rather have prescribed hellebore than hemlock." As in all other cases his purpose is to make the reader skeptical of the arguments of religious fanatics.

FRANCIS BACON

The third and greatest intellectual giant of the period is Francis Bacon. It is acknowledged that his character was not equal to his intellect and we do not look to him for clear and consistent judgments on the creeds of his time, especially as Protestantism still for a time showed itself as prone to light fires in the market place or chop off heads as the Roman church. Elizabeth, who was herself a skeptic (see my Biographical Dictionary) and at first averse from persecution, was driven to it by Catholic conspiracies, and her Protestant divines wanted the old law "On the Burning of a Heretic" extended to all skeptics. Yet I may observe in passing that while religious writers still gladly quote contemptuous jibes at Atheism from one of Bacon's essays the Atheist could quote from another a defense of his position and a refutation of the chief argument that is now used against it. In Essay XVI "On Atheism," he says:

"I would rather believe all the fables in the Legend of the Talmud or the Alcoran (the Koran) than that this universal frame is without a mind. And therefore God never wrought miracles to convince Atheism because this order doth convince it. It is true that a little philosophy inclineth man's mind to Atheism but depth in philosophy bringeth men's minds back to religion."

I might claim that the second part of this passage, which he repeats in his great work "The Advancement of Learning," might be quoted as a specimen of the dumbness of the great. It was as true then as it is now that those who come to the deliberate conclusion that the existence of God is not proved are, class for class, apt to be more thoughtful and more diligent readers than the believers. When Professor Leuba made a confidential inquiry, by getting personal testimonies, into beliefs in American universities, he found ("The Belief in God and Immortality," 1921) that less than 10 percent of the students were Atheists, while 49 percent of the ordinary professors of science and 65 percent of the more eminent professors had no belief in God; and a repetition of the inquiry in 1934 showed that Atheism had increased among the more learned. But the chief point to note here is that when it became a widespread belief that knowledge, particularly of science, led to Atheism, the cry was raised that it would have dire social consequences. In the very next essay Bacon replies with great strength to this argument. The essay, "On Superstition," begins:

"It were better to have no God at all than such an opinion as is unworthy of him. For the one is unbelief, the other contumely; and certainly superstition is the reproach of the Deity . . . And as the contumely is the greater towards God so the danger is greater towards men. Atheism leaves a man to sense, to philosophy, to natural piety, to laws, to reputation; all which may be guides to an outward moral virtue though religion were not; but superstition dismantles all these and createth an absolute monarchy in the minds of men. Therefore Atheism did never perturb states, for it makes men wary of themselves, as looking no further; and we see the times inclined to Atheism (as the time of Augustus Caesar) were civil times. But superstition hath been the confusion of many states and bringeth in a new *primum mobile* that ravisheth all the spheres of government . . . Superstition without a veil is a deformed thing, for as it addeth deformity to an ape to be so like a man so the similitude of superstition to religion maketh it the more depraved."

You may find this useful to quote against your Catholic friend whose religion Bacon had in mind when, arguing about "Communistic Atheism," he glibly quotes Bacon's jibe at Atheism.

But what chiefly concerns us here is whether, in view of Bacon's high position in the history of science, we shall find in his works none of the absurdities that still linger in the works of Bodin. As a matter of fact, Bacon's position in science has often been challenged in modern times. I do not refer to those Catholic writers who foolishly say that Roger Bacon (whose entire learning came from the Spanish Arabs) ought to take the place of Francis, for he had no influence on the development of science. Draper described Lord Bacon as "a pretender in science, a time-serving politician, an insidious lawyer, a treacherous friend, and a bad man." He persistently rejected the Copernican theory, the greatest discovery (or recovery from ancient Greek science) of his time; and the article on him in the responsible British Dictionary of National Biography observes that he was "not fully abreast of the scientific knowledge of the day." He never mentions Harvey's discovery of the circulation of the blood or the astronomical discoveries of Kepler, and the so-called "Baconian method" of scientific investigation provokes the smiles of the modern scientist. He believed in astrology, alchemy, and magic. In his "Advancement of Learning" he follows "Genesis" with simple credulity and makes some ingenuous reflections on the narrative such as:

"The first acts which man performed in Paradise consist of two summary parts of knowledge: the view of the psychology of creatures and the imposition of names."

The "Advancement" is considered the greatest work of science before the 18th century, yet it discusses Eden, the Flood, the Tower of Babel, Moses, Solomon, and the Prophets as solemnly as a Sunday-school book.

It incidentally praises the abominable book in which King James I had affirmed his fanatical zeal against witchcraft:

"Your Majesty doth excellently well observe that witchcraft is the height of Idolatry."

He was poor in mathematics. "Mathematics I hold to be a branch of metaphysics," he says; he either could not follow or was ignorant of important advances in physics and mechanics that were made in his time by Galileo and others; and he did not know of the precession of the equinoxes. He held that air and water are mutually convertible in certain conditions, and that spring-waters come from the condensation of air in underground caverns. He believed that air had no weight, and that lightness is a positive quality of some bodies: that phosphorescence on the sea is due to violent strokes of the oar: that the moon may be simply a mass of illuminated vapor, that "cold contracts every substance" (in spite of his familiarity with ice) : that "the heart of an ape applied to the head helpeth the wit and is good for falling sickness:" that bracelets may, according to their action, be divided into "refrigerant, corroborative, and apperient:" and that the application of mathematics degrades astronomy.

There is, in fine, a small Latin work of his, "The Wisdom of the Ancients," that might be called a howler from beginning to end. It finds an occult and deep wisdom in all the myths and fables of the ancient world. He takes, for instance, the outrageous legend of the giant Typhon, a bastard of Juno and the Earth, who fights and beats Jupiter and carries away his sinews until Mercury steals and restores them. "This fable," he says, "seems to point to the variable fortunes of princes and the rebellious insurrection of traitors in a state." In the figure of Pan we have "the body of Nature elegantly and with deep judgment depainted hairy, representing the beams of operations of creatures; for beams are, as it were, the hairs and bristles of Nature." Mme. Blavatsky and Mrs. Besant would have found the little book a treasure-house, but admirers of Bacon have never ventured to translate it.

VII.   ABERRATIONS OF EARLY SCIENCE

If we are tempted to be more ironical when we read the blunders of these theologians than when we find scientific men or sociologists going astray it is easy to find the reason. The theologian pretends that he is reading a message of supreme clearness, the Word of God, as he calls it; and when his reading of it leads him into such moral crudities as those I have quoted from Luther we cannot forget that the same documents are still pressed upon the world as its wisest guidance. The early man of science has a far higher claim to our leniency. He is trying to read below the surface of nature, and it necessarily took ages for man to develop his own capability to do this, to create the technique of science. It was just because these pioneers first tried the blundering interpretations of nature, century after century, that our modern age finds itself upon the right path.

COPERNICUS

We saw that that was true of Bacon, but he was not so much a scientific worker as a humanist whose great task was to convince the world that it would profit enormously if it fired its theologians and philosophers and enlisted the services of men of science or of "the new knowledge." So perversely are these things written in our time that most people suppose that Copernicus had, before the time of Bacon, cut a genuine scientific path through the thickets of medieval ignorance and based his discovery of the central position of the sun upon a mass of direct observations of nature. This misrepresentation of the work of Copernicus—not by distinguished astronomers or historians of science, be it noted—is largely due to the idea, which responsible scientists sometimes repeat, that he was a "devout Polish priest." He was never a priest (though for the sake of the revenue a canon), was decidedly not a devout puritan, and was not strictly speaking a Pole.

But the main point is that any expert work will tell you that, while he later had an observatory and studied the heavens, he borrowed the idea which we call Copernicanism from the ancient Greeks. At the age of 23 he went to study in Italy. In the north-Italian cities Frederick the Great had successfully planted the seeds of Arab science while Rome remained backward and despised, and Copernicus found that his professor at Bologna and others more or less secretly held what they called the Pythagorean theory—that the sun is the center of the solar system—against the Ptolemaic. He at once (or certainly before 1512) accepted it. Yet it was not until 1543 that his book on the theory appeared, and not until he was safe in the grave from the long arm of the Inquisition. The point does not properly concern me here but in view of modern talk about the "devout priest" and his wonderful scientific genius it is useful to know that this was no discovery but the restoration to life of an ancient Greek theory. As to the modern claim that the Church was so far from obstructing scientific research that it allowed Copernicus to lecture in Rome—the degenerate Pope of his time would in any case not be in the least interested—the "secrecy" with which the north-Italian astronomers held the theory, the 30 years delay of Copernicus in publishing it, and his nervous fear to publish while he lived are significant enough. If there is any appearance of leniency in his time as compared with that of Galileo, remember that the Jesuit Society had not yet been founded. Their "tolerant" Church kept the famous book of Copernicus on the Index for 200 years after all science accepted his theory and it was as clearly true as the rotundity of the earth.

What it is more pertinent to notice here is that once Copernicus learned from the Greeks that the sun is the center of the solar system and began on his own account to work out the structure of that system he blundered like his predecessors. He kept the metaphysical idea of Aristotle that the paths of the planets must be perfect circles, and he invented such a system of cycles within cycles that the sun, some astronomers say, was not really central. Professor Forbes gives a lot of space in his short "History of Astronomy" to Copernicus with the sole object of proving—and he is himself a religious writer—that it was Kepler not Copernicus whose name ought to be given to the system, and that Copernicus' theory of the solar system was totally wrong.

Others found out that if you look beyond the solar system to the universe he blundered as badly as his predecessors. Columbia University has published a translation of his "First Narration," and you will find his conception of the universe hopelessly medieval. He believed in the old solid firmament decorated with pretty little stars like a Christmas ceiling:

"The sphere of the stars, which we call the eighth sphere, was created by God to be the region which would enclose within its confines the entire realm of nature (the solar system), and hence it was fixed and immovable on the plane of the universe . . . Hence this sphere was studded by God for our sake with a large number of twinkling stars in order that by comparison with them, securely fixed in place, we might observe the positions and motions of the other enclosed spheres and planets." (143.)

Beyond this firmament there is nothing for man to investigate he says, "except in so far as Holy Writ has vouchsafed us knowledge." These numerous and comprehensive blunders we, as I said, expect to find in the pioneers, especially pioneers of science before the telescope was invented, but we must set them against the undue glorification of Copernicus as one of the "great Catholic scientists." He had not the pure scientific spirit. He repeatedly warns his readers that we must not depart from the teaching of antiquity unless we are compelled by strong evidence.

TYCHO BRAHE

The first really great astronomer, in the sense of relying upon personal and assiduous observation, after the Arabs was Tycho Brahe the Dane, a Protestant (1546-1601). He made a number of discoveries, such as that, contrary to the prevailing belief, comets do not arise from the earth (as fiery exhalations). But he was totally wrong about the solar system. Instead of developing the main theory advocated by Copernicus he adopted a clumsy compromise between it and the Ptolemaic system. He made the earth stationary with the sun and moon circling round it, while the other planets revolved round the sun and the spheres of fixed stars revolved round the whole. Many astronomers believe that it was out of fear of the church—as I said, the Reformers rejected Copernicanism as scornfully as the Popes did—that Brahe restored the earth to its central position while others consider that he had not the intellectual power to master his material, but Eisles shows in a recent work "The Royal Art of Astrology," that he found that astrological forecasts were impossible unless the earth was fixed and central; and Tycho Brahe believed in astrology as firmly as any Pope.

KEPLER

Brahe had left behind a large and chaotic mass of recorded observations, and it was largely on the strength of these that his pupil Kepler, a more brilliant thinker, worked out the true scheme, on broad lines, of the solar system and laid the first foundation of modern astronomy. But he was, like his master, repeatedly led astray by his mysticism. At first he believed that in a universe of such beauty and harmony—it was the time of the ghastly Thirty Years War!—the path of a planet round the sun must be a circle (the perfect figure). Observations compelled him to change to eclipses, but his mysticism moved him to connect the movements of the heavenly bodies with musical intervals in a completely fantastic theory. The ex-monk Giordano Bruno had adopted the view of the Ionian Greeks that the stars were vast bodies at great distances from the earth; that, in fact, the universe consisted of an infinite number of such bodies in some sort of eternal evolution. Kepler quotes and rejects, clearly under religious influence, this theory of the stars. He, in fact, wasted a good deal of his time in computing and writing a book on "The True Year in Which Christ was Born."

GALILEO

. Galileo, who was primarily a physicist though his conflicts with the Church have made him best known as an astronomer, came next. From the discovery of a Dutch optician that two spectacle-lenses placed together in a certain position would magnify distant objects he constructed the first real telescope and lifted his science to a higher plane, besides himself making many discoveries. One of his chief services was to establish for all time the central position of the sun, in spite of the fact that in his old age and under the threats of the Roman Inquisition he insincerely disavowed that view. Apart from this, however, he made many serious blunders. He refused to admit Tycho Brahe's theory of comets and encouraged the world in the fantastic view that they were exhalations from the earth. He ignored Kepler's greatest discovery—'

that of the laws of the solar system—and clearly from conceit, took no notice of the discoveries of several other scientific rivals. It is necessary to point out these defects if we take any notice of the blunders of pioneers, though Galileo's work was so great and his fate so tragic that no one cares to criticize him.

SIR ISAAC NEWTON

Greatest genius of all these pioneers of science was Sir Isaac Newton (1660-1726), yet no great scientist since the Middle Ages was diverted by his religious views into so many absurdities. It is often said in extenuation that he drifted into his Bible-founded absurdities in his old age, but the British Dictionary of National Biography explains that "his theological writings were begun at an early period of his life," and that at the age of 30 he was counted an "excellent divine." Whether these studies led him into a rejection of the Trinity, as there is good reason to believe, they certainly had results that astonish us in the case of so great a genius. A divine not far removed from his age says of him:

"This truly great and good man applied himself with the utmost attention to the study of the holy scriptures and considered the several parts of them with uncommon exactness; particularly as to the years of time and the series of prophecies and events relating to the Messiah . . . he proved that the prophecy in Daniel's work was an express prophecy of the coming of the Messiah."

This will be to most folk a new conception of the famous mathematician and one of the greatest scientists of all time, but the work survives, and I have read it, in which he solemnly records his fantastic conclusions ("Observations on the Prophecies of Daniel"). Of all the prophets, he says. "Daniel is the most distinct in order of time and easiest to be understood." We know today, of course, that the work is a late and clumsy forgery, and there never was a prophet Daniel. Speaking of Nature as "the world natural" and history as "the world politic," he says:

"Accordingly the whole world natural, consisting of the heavens and the earth, signifies the whole world politic, consisting of thrones, and the things in that world signify the analogous thrones and dignities and those who enjoy them, and the earth, with the things therein, the inferior people, and the lowest parts of the earth called Hades or Hell, the lowest or most miserable part of them."

There is no need to quote the fantastic things to which this line of reasoning conducted the great scientist.

Another outcome of this adulteration of his thoughts with mysticism was a pseudo-historical book based upon the Old Testament and a rich collection of legends and fables, which he called "The Chronology of Ancient Kingdoms." Here is a sample:

"Melchisedech was a priest of the Most High God and Abraham solemnly bowed to him, which he would scarce have done had they not been of one and the same religion."

Which must have surprised the divines. The Egyptians, whose civilization began, he says, about 1200 B.C., "boasted that it was thousands of years older than the world, and that Ammon, Osiris, Bacchus, and Hercules were Kings of theirs." The Greeks were contemporaries of the Egyptians, and the Argonauts were the sons of Bacchus. Isis was a Greek woman taken by the Egyptians when they conquered Greece. In short, this product of the studies of a genius is a clotted mass of nonsense.

With the eccentricities of smaller, though in their day esteemed gifted, men many chapters could be filled. The zeal for science and defiance of authority and tradition were quickening the brains of men where the Great War of Catholics and Protestants had not laid the earth waste or the Inquisition did not put its bloody penalties on free thinking. Leonardo da Vinci had correctly guessed the meaning of fossils but the old ideas prevailed. Even the great anatomist Fallopio said that they were just concretions that were due to putrefaction in the rocks. Tycho Brahe's theory of comets fared little better. The whole learned world was at one time agitated over a theory that there were men living on the earth before Adam, but this monstrous supposition was buried under mounds of scorn and, in the old medieval manner the marvellous wisdom and power of Adam were again discussed. A new theory of volcanoes—that the fires were due to beds of coal with sulphur burning between—got wide attention, and a "powder of sympathy" which cured wounds if you applied it to the sword that had caused them, or even to rags taken from the wound, was widely treasured. But the list of superstitions of even the 17th century would be lengthy, and we will here again confine ourselves to "the dumbness of the great."

SIR WILLIAM HARVEY

A great figure in medicine was Sir William Harvey, the discoverer of the circulation of the blood. Aristotle's idea was that the food was converted into blood in the liver and proceeded into the veins from the heart, and that the arteries had nothing to do with the blood so there was no circulation. This, with few modifications, was the received doctrine in medicine and surgery until the 17th century. Indeed a writer of the time says that when Harvey, a distinguished physician, announced his discovery, "he fell mightily in his practice and it was believed by the vulgar that he was crackbrained and all physicians were against him." As Harvey could not, from lack of the microscope, know anything about the capillaries, the fine hair-like vessels which enable the blood to pass from the arteries to the vains, he could not explain the circulation but he established the fact.

In connection with his second great discovery, however, he started some new and serious errors. The origin and embryonic development of an animal remained little better understood than it had been after Aristotle's work on the subject, and it was still universally believed that whole classes of the lower animals—worms, marine organisms, insects, etc.—were produced, without any parents, from the action of the sun on slime and muck. Harvey got from the royal forests 12 does that had been with the buck, and he dissected them one after the other, at intervals, in order to study the development of the embryo. He concluded that "every living thing comes from an egg," which began the reaction against the age-old superstition of spontaneous generation, but as he could not possibly prove this in the reputed cases of spontaneous generation, that belief lasted even in science until the middle of the 19th century. But as the embryo is too minute to be seen with the naked eye in the earliest stages, or so minute that it is easily missed, he concluded that the male's spermatic fluid does not reach the womb but emits a vapor which stimulates the womb to secrete an egg. It would be a long time before the advance of the microscope enabled scientific men to discover the ovum and the spermatozoon, and still longer before the early embryonic process was even broadly understood. A philosopher of the 17th century, Malebranche won the attention of all Europe for his theory that the ovum is an infinitesimally small man which merely grows larger and larger in the womb: so small that Mother Eve contained in her ovaries the whole future race in miniature.

DESCARTES

The French philosopher Descartes (1596-1650) was one of the most original and most brilliant thinkers of his age in physics, mathematics, and metaphysics, and he paid the usual penalty of pioneering by stumbling into many errors. In the case of able men whose blunders I quote at this period one must remember the environment. Not only was the art of discovering truth in your inner consciousness or in the intangible ether (metaphysics) decaying and men were beginning to look at Nature in a new fashion but the appalling clash of Catholic and Protestant convulsed all Europe. Descartes pursued his studies during the Thirty Years War and became himself a soldier. But the conflict of opinions obsessed his mind, and he proposed to find a new method and a new basis for attaining certainty. He chose as the criterion of truth clearness of vision, practically intuition, and mathematics as the basis of a new structure of knowledge. His famous starting point after sweeping aside all received opinions and authority, "I think therefore I exist," was soon known all over Europe and is widely known today.

But it is a fallacy, and the method of establishing it is fallacious. Even modern psychology labors hard to explain this "I" or personality, and all that Descartes was justified in claiming on his own criterion was that "thought (or thinking) exists." The criterion was bad because, for instance, the mystic will tell you that the clearest idea in his mind is the reality of God. Applying his method to the existence of God and the distinction between a material (or "extended" or measurable) body and a spiritual ("unextended" or not measurable) entity easily—much too easily—gave Descartes back his religious beliefs. As a matter of fact, he had never really parted with them, and they profoundly influenced his choice of a method which was supposed to guide him in his search. Descartes rendered a service in his sharp distinction between the material and the spiritual, for every attempt of a modern thinker to define them differently fails or is hopelessly vague, but his whole philosophy is unsound and it to some extent spoiled his services to science. His explanation of physical movement was fantastic. Bodies do not move because they are pushed but from something in their own nature:

"A body that you see rise and fall as if it were seeking its soul comes to rest when it reaches its proper place because it is reunited with its form."

I should note, however, that he took up the ancient Greek idea, adopted by Giordano Bruno, of the evolution of worlds and gave a suggestive (naturally inaccurate) theory of the evolution of the solar system.

In biology or physiology he again rendered a great service and made notable blunders. Cardano had said that the whole of nature was animated. Descartes was the first since the Greek Materialists to reject the idea that there was an immaterial principle even in the plant and the animal. A witty French lady of the time illustrated it by saying that according to M. Descartes a machine which we call a dog mounts a machine which we call a bitch and presently there is a little machine which we call a puppy. Seriously, it was a considerable service to drive the immaterial out of the whole universe except man and claim that all organic life below the level of thought is mechanical. The bolder French thinkers of the next century, rejecting his arbitrary criterion of truth, went on logically to drive the spirit from its last citadel, the pineal body, in which Descartes had located the soul. He allowed, of course, that the purely animal functions of even the human body were mechanical, though he blundered a lot about them. For instance, he denied that the circulation is due to "the expansion of the blood caused by the heat of the heart." He accepted too, the old idea that "animal spirits" in the nerves convey impressions or sensations to the body in the center of the brain and a number of other crude ideas. But perhaps his service in extending the realm of Materialism as far as the very threshold of consciousness outweighs all these.

PIERRE GASSENDI

His contemporary Pierre Gassendi (1592-1655), who was not only a Catholic (though suspected and persecuted) like Descartes but a priest, is not often mentioned today. He is not included in the list of "great Catholic scientists." And that is because he innocently provided another foundation of modern Materialism by restoring to favor the philosophy of Epicurus. Doubtless he took literally the Greek tradition, in fact the teaching of Lucretius, that Epicurus believed that there were gods somewhere in the universe. However that may be, he tried to blend Epicureanism with Christianity, and as he was a fine mathematician and a man of notable ability he had an influence comparable to that of Descartes. A school of real Epicureans, without the mysticism of Gassendi, was formed in Paris. The great comedian Moliere belonged to it. Gassendi made a few unimportant discoveries, but his outstanding service to science was that he fiercely attacked the devotion to Aristotle and brought back the theory that matter is composed of atoms which Aristotle had rejected. We should probably find that John Dalton, who finally established atomism in science a century and a half later, was indebted to him. In psychology also he was useful in advocating that all real knowledge comes, ultimately, through the senses. But in detail his works are full of such things as these:

"When an apple decays it is changing into worms.

"A handful of iron cannot be produced from a handful of snow because of the scarcity of material.

"A vacuum cannot exist because matter would have to be destroyed."

PASCAL

Of the third great French mathematician of the time, Pascal, it is not necessary to speak. He figures prominently in the history of mathematics but he admitted all sorts of crude errors in other branches of science. His predominant interest was in religion yet hardly any but a modern mystic now reads his famous "Thoughts on Religion." Modern divines do not like his two most famous sayings: "The heart hath its reasons which the reason knoweth not" and "You must bet." Indifferentism and "the open mind" in regard to religion were growing. You *must* takes sides, said Pascal; or, in plainer French, put your money on religion. Most of the indifferentists just asked: Why?

VIII.   THE GREAT MODERN PHILOSOPHERS

The record of philosophy covers two periods of man's history: the Greek period and, with a medieval interlude in which the Christian Schoolmen and the Arabs feebly revived Aristotle, the modern period. Anybody who knows the history of thought will be tempted to feel that when the authority of Aristotle fell at last before the assaults of such men as Bacon, Galileo, and Newton yet the path to truth by way of scientific observation yielded profit so slowly, men of high intellectual vitality turned again to try the metaphysical short-cut. The philosopher, of course, will not admit that philosophy is a short cut. He holds, as Aristotle did, that it studies aspects of things that are not seen by the scientific eye. However that may be, the attempt to learn truth by speculation instead of observation and analysis of observations began in the 17th century, and it affords a large number of what anybody but a metaphysician will call absurdities.

HOBBES

I have already shown how Descartes' attempt to create a philosophy distorted his gift for physical speculation, as we find in his brilliant, though necessarily crude, attempt to account for the origin of the solar

48

system and his firm belief that all life below the level of thought is purely mechanical. His British contemporary Hobbes (1588-1679) is more apt to be classed amongst the philosophers. Of purely metaphysical speculation, it is true, he knew little and cared less. He is best remembered as a political thinker, and as such he blundered heroically. The Renaissance or revival of classical literature had led to much study of Plato in England, and many had learned from him to cherish the idea of a republic. This had not a little to do with the Civil War, at the close of which Englishmen had the proud distinction of being the first nation in modern times to cut off the head of a king. In this troubled time fell the philosophizing of Hobbes. He was a man of such ability that he had begun to study Latin and Greek at the age of 6, and he was only 13 when he translated the great Greek tragedy "Medea" into Latin verse. He was a man of prodigious learning, and he conceived the idea of organizing all knowledge in a three-volume system of, broadly, physical science, human science (or psychology), and practical science (sociology).

In physical science he just reproduced the errors of his age, but he tentatively broke new ground in psychology and prepared the way for the revolutionary theory that all man's knowledge must begin with his sense-perceptions (or, in modern language, presentations). Even here he was entangled in old errors. While the nerves generally conveyed to the brain the impressions of senses got from the external world, he said, some of them went to the heart instead of the brain, and they gave rise to a man's emotions and feelings of pleasure or pain. We may say at least for him that in denying that there was any other source of human knowledge than the formation by the brain of "conceptions" based entirely upon the data of sense he, in spite of his deliberate vagueness about the religious idea of mind, brought thinking men away from mysticism and in the proper direction for research. Similarly in regard to moral ideas: he professed religion but in some places clearly says that the good is what gives pleasure and the evil what inflicts pain. But his most definite and worst blunder was in political philosophy. Here he was, his chief biographer says, "a sublimely one-sided thinker." He was not only a timid man, shrinking from the troubles of his age, but by profession the tutor of aristocratic pupils —even of Charles II in his youth—and he emphatically argued that royalty is essential to a civilization. Political writers had already begun to speak of "the social compact." It could only be, said Hobbes, a compact of subjects to obey the king.

JOHN LOCKE

His psychological hint was his greatest service, and John Locke, next in the line of British thinkers (1632-1704) developed this. His greatest work was his "Essay on the Understanding," the fruit of long years spent in examining and analyzing his mind. It may justly be called one of the foundations of modern psychology. You might, in fact, say that just as the astronomers were making an intelligible cosmos out of the weird conception of the universe that had hitherto ruled men's minds, Locke began the work of making an intelligible system of the mind. But, like Hobbes, he was often diverted by the pressure of religion. His famous saying, "There is nothing in the intellect that did not reach it through the senses"—mystics thought they were clever in adding "except the intellect itself," but Locke had allowed for that— led logically to a denial of all intuition, moral or intellectual, yet he speaks at times of our "intuitive knowledge," and he completely failed on the ethical side. Christianity alone, he said, could provide some of our moral sentiments. Ethical systems before Christ were of little value. Speaking of the idea of working out a naturalistic theory and code of morals, he says: "It would seem from the little that has hitherto been done in it that it is too hard a task for unassisted reason to establish morality in all its parts, at least for the common people, and the Gospel contains so perfect a body of ethics that reason may be excused from that inquiry." He insists that for any morality at all there must be freedom of the will, and that for "common people" to be moral they must continue to believe in heaven and hell. But his references to the common people do not mean that he shared the political philosophy of Hobbes. He interpreted the "social compact" more reasonably and concluded that the body of the citizens were free to adopt a republican form of government.

In the case of these two British thinkers we have a perception of sound and important principles which would, with full recognition of their debt to Locke, be boldly developed by British and French thinkers of the 18th century, but they are driven into absurdities of principle and fact by the religious pressure of the times. It was worse with contemporaries of Locke on the continent of Europe whose names are included in histories of philosophy. Particularly absurd—so absurd that one wonders why it aroused so much interest and survives at all in modern literature—was the system of the French thinker, a priest, Malebranche. It is sometimes described as "the system of Descartes modified by the teaching of St. Augustine." Descartes' theories were so widely defended yet so bitterly assailed by the Jesuits that this priest felt that he must bring them into harmony with Christian teaching. In sharply defining matter as "extended substance" (measurable) and spirit as unextended Descartes had made more acute than ever the difficulty of understanding how, in man, one could act upon the other. They do not, Malebranche said. The mind does not even perceive matter as Hobbes and Locke had contended. All movement in matter comes from God, and he causes a corresponding movement in the mind. In fact, matter cannot even act on matter. To put it in a more familiar form than the priest would, his view was that when you are playing billiards and you smack the white against the red it is not this shock that makes the second ball roll over the table. All movement is from God. A clap of thunder is not the cause of the sensation you have. It is only the "occasion" of your sensation. A German doodlebug did not destroy a building. We just see the two events together or in close sequence because we see everything in the divine-mind. This fantastic creed, called Occasionalism, is still treated quite respectfully in manuals of the history of philosophy.

SPINOZA

Naturally it leads logically to the belief that God and nature are one reality, as the contemporary Spinoza taught and, be it said, Malebranche, as an orthodox priest, flatly denied. I will not include Spinoza's Pantheism amongst our absurdities, though to call it, as is customary, "a sublime conception" is certainly an absurdity. As in the case of the immensely greater intellect of Goethe and with all respect to that intellect, Pantheism (which was well known in ancient Greece for the same reason) became from the time of Spinoza an area of refuge for skeptics who for one reason or other dreaded to be called Atheists. Today they have the more respectable refuge of Agnosticism. But I need not point out the absurdities of the system. Spinoza adopted Descartes' definition of matter and spirit, which makes them flatly contradictory of each other and irreconcilable yet made material nature and the spiritual God one being. Philosophical verbiage might seem to get over this difficulty but when you come down to earth and reflect on all its unpleasant features—wars, poverty, cruelty, sewage systems, gluttony, crime, etc.—you do not seriously discuss Pantheism or its equivalent, the theory that everything that seems to have a material existence really exists only in the mind of God. I will show later that that was the real creed of two men who were idolized in our modern religious world for years, Sir James Jeans and Sir Arthur Eddington. In fact, modern historians of philosophy who do not even mention D'Alembert, Diderot, and Helvetius, devote 12 pages to Spinoza, eight to Berkeley (the chief representative of the all-in-the-mind-of-God theory) and eight to Leibnitz. So the Rationalist Benn's "History of Modern Philosophy." Then they rebuke us Materialists for being so disrespectful to philosophy.

LEIBNITZ

Leibnitz (1646-1716), being contemporary with Malebranche in the period which was still discussing Descartes, was confronted with the same problem, how to bridge the gulf between spirit and matter. After all, nature is a panorama of movement a good part of which is said to be spiritual or immaterial, and the power of mind (or soul) over body was held to be as obvious a fact as gravitation or the influence on the mind of drugs or whiskey. The German philosopher Leibnitz was convinced that he had settled the problem forever; and he had one of the most powerful intellects in Europe in his day. He read Latin easily and was learning Greek at the age of 11, he entered the university at 15, and he was never a parson; he was in fact a statesman of outstanding ability. All Europe listened—the Queen of England at the time was one of his pupils—when the oracle delivered the solution of the riddle of the universe; and it was as fantastic as that of Malebranche.

The universe does not consist of the atoms of the materialists but of infinitesimally small units which he called "monads." They were more or less like mathematical points, having no extension in space; something, in fact, like what some modern physicists call "centers of force." God is the Big Monad, and then you get all sorts down to the monads which make up a bit of matter; though this is largely an illusion or "phenomenal." The monads are all endowed with activity but they never act on each other. "The monads," he says, "have no windows by which anything can go in and out." It is not the sight of a film-star's nude thighs that opens the little valves in a good man's cheek and lets the blood flow to it or gives a feeling of pleasure to the wicked man; nor is it your excess in thinking or drinking that gives you a headache. (Leibnitz did not say this, but it is a correct application of his system.) One bunch of monads, the body, cannot have any action whatever on the soul-monad, and vice versa.

Then, you ask, what the heck . . . "It is all explained by Pre-established Harmony. The two sets of monads, material and spiritual, may be imagined as two great clocks which were set to the same time by God on creation's morn. So if in the year 1948 you burn your fingers you have an exactly appropriate feeling in your spiritual monad. The two clocks will keep exactly the same time—your material lesion coinciding with the spiritual feeling—throughout the ages. And if you raise the difficulty that your body did not even exist on creation's morn Leibnitz has a reply. It did. We—all humans to the end of time—were packed—tiny, of course—in Mother Eve's ovary. To God all things are possible. He is a great help to apologists. What is even more surprising is that Leibnitz looked out upon the world as his philosophy made it and declared that of all possible or conceivable worlds this on which we live is the best. Since every little movement in it was predestined by the Almighty when he created it, how could it be otherwise? Germany at the time had not yet recovered from a war which in some ways was worse than our modern wars. But what are facts to a philosopher?

I trust that the reader does not imagine that, because I dislike philosophy I am trying to discredit it by selecting a few obscure or not important thinkers of the 17th and 18th centuries. On the contrary I choose the men who occupy most space and are accorded the greatest respect at this period in historics of philosophy. Leibnitz was, as I said, one of the greatest figures of his time. Next to him the historian of philosophy takes Bishop Berkeley, who genially explained—and was taken seriously—that there is no such thing as a material universe and so no problem of the relations of matter and spirit to worry about (and, of course, no wars, atomic bombs, poverty, syphilis, sewers, whores, drunkards, rapers, etc.)—these are just ideas in the mind of God.

DAVID HUME

They then discuss the famous Scottish scholar and historian, David Hume (1711-76), the friend of Rousseau. There is a ground of some actual interest for glancing at his system. When the more wicked skeptics suggest that many in our time are mainly moved by a desire for respectability when they call themselves "Agnostics" instead of "Atheists," the reply is that when Professor Huxley founded Agnosticism he based it upon a solid philosophical theory, that of Hume, which prevents any but a superficial or ignorant man from calling himself an Atheist. Following up the discovery of Locke, that our real knowledge is the formation of conceptions from the messages which the sense-organs send to the mind or brain, Hume made a searching inquiry into the nature of this mechanism.

People—the overwhelming majority—who never give a thought to these matters have no idea of the tremendous difficulty of explaining what knowledge is and how what we call the mind can know or perceive anything outside itself. When we smile at the conclusions of these philosophers we must remember these difficulties, which the scientist passes over by assuming that our sense-presentations and ideas do represent an external world. It is still a thorny problem. Berkeley and the "idealists," concluded that we cannot get beyond the mind: that, therefore, the existence of a material world is an illusion. Hume concluded that these messages from the senses (vision, odors, tastes, touch, pain, etc.) are certainly from an external world, but that on Locke's principle that there is nothing in the intellect that did not come from the senses; we can have no certain knowledge of anything besides what the senses actually announce (color, shapes, odors, etc.) Common sense—the Scottish philosophers characteristically recognized this as an instrument of knowledge—insists that there must be realities outside the mind that cause these sensations but we can't know them. We know our "states of consciousness"—the contents of our mind—and nothing more. Whether there is a God corresponding to our idea of one, and so on, we have no equipment to learn.

This idealism—we know ideas only, not things or realities—is the theoretical basis of Agnosticism as it was formulated by Huxley. It seems so preposterous that a reader must ask himself how far either Hume or Huxley really believed it. On the theory a man cannot know even that he has a body, much less a soul, yet Hume was a great historian, telling his readers how realities (nations and individuals) had behaved long before his own consciousness existed. He was also one of the ablest formulators of the naturalistic theory of morality. Huxley was one of the ablest physiologists of the time, and in religious controversy he discussed what Jesus did or did not do 1,900 years ago as seriously as any realist. He said that Hume's discoveries meant that he had no power to say anything at all, positive or negative, about this idea of a God or the meaning and nature of life and so on. But he handled the arguments for the existence of God and the immortality of the soul as critically as any Atheist did, and he did more than any in his time to establish the mechanical nature of life. Modern Agnostics do not even profess to follow Hume; in fact—and I have probably met more of them than any other man—I question if one in 100 of them could tell what Hume's theory was.

Even to those of us who do realize the serious difficulty that still exists in trying to explain knowledge—in my own opinion it will not be .

solved until the physiology and anatomy of the brain are enormously advanced beyond their present condition—this philosophical attempt at a solution seems to be a greater absurdity than the errors of earlier observers or thinkers about the ways of animals or the structure of the body or the universe. Yet it may be said to have dominated philosophy or all "profound" thinkers until the 20th century; and even philosophers like Bertrand Russell who are supposed to have introduced realism and sanity into philosophy do not go nearly as far as the realism of the man of science or the common man.

KANT

The next great figure in the history of philosophy after Leibnitz is Kant (1724-1804), and he was not only generally believed for a quarter of a century to have said the last word on the theory of knowledge but you find him still mentioned in our literature as if he were the Aristotle of modern times. In any history of philosophy you will find four men standing out as the most profound of all thinkers—Plato and Aristotle in ancient times and Kant and Hegel in modern times. And the chief reason is because all four were emphatic anti-Materialists.

Kant was certainly a man of high intellectual power but he had just the temperament to follow the idealistic line of his predecessors. He lived a solitary, broody life—pupils of his said that during a lecture he kept his eyes on a particular button of a particular student's coat and they one day upset him by cutting it off—and, after an early stage in which he was interested in astronomy, he lived entirely in the world of his own "states of consciousness." No one now followed Descartes in his fantastic theory that the soul or mind dwelt in the pineal body—a little nut-shaped body, possibly an atrophied eye, in the center of the brain—but they almost as mischievously conceived the mind as a separate entity working through a part of the brain, and so the problem of explaining how it could know anything "outside itself" remained as acute as ever. Kant followed Hume and Locke as far as sense-impressions were concerned, except that he held that time and space are subjective "forms" into which the material of the sense-impressions was molded. His famous original work was to conclude that the reason or intelligence itself had from its own nature a number of such subjective forms, like the pigeon-holes in a businessman's desk, in which his perceptions automatically sort themselves out. Causality, for instance or the idea of cause and effect, is one of these forms. It followed that it was an illusion to imagine that we perceived causes and effects outside ourselves, and therefore all attempts to prove the existence of God by the argument for a First Cause or a chain of causes in nature is a sheer fallacy. In short, all elements of rational thought, or all mental activity above the level of sense-perception, are purely subjective. It is just the nature of mind to conceive things that way.

There were thus, according to Kant, two sorts of existence or realities: phenomena (objects of sense) and noumena (objects of thought). We could know phenomena but not noumena. I told in an earlier chapter how Aristotle distinguished two sorts of realities, accidents (shapes, colors, odors, etc.) and substances (the underlying realities); as if nature had more or less the structure of a nut with its kernel (the substance of a thing) hidden in a shell of accidents. No one except a Catholic theologian, who uses this musty old piece of metaphysics to explain the magic of converting bread and wine into the body of Christ while they continue to look, feel and taste like bread and wine, takes any notice today of this idea. But Kant's phenomena and noumena are pretty much the same thing under new names. He had so profound an influence that all through the 19th century it was commonly said that science studies phenomena or the phenomenal universe and leaves the noumena to religion and philosophy. Strictly speaking it was just as much a basis for Skepticism or Agnosticism as Hume's theory was. God and all spiritual things are noumena. The mind can play with the ideas but cannot say whether there are realities corresponding to them.

To complete what most of us moderns would call the absurdity Kant distinguished two different faculties of reason: pure reason and practical reason. The satirical writer Richter put it in a sort of parable. Kant, he said, had an idol in his study which his old servant Lampe (taken as a representative or allegory of Demos, the people) greatly venerated. Lampe came in one morning to find that his master had broken up the idol and, to put an end to his tears, Kant had to find a way of restoring the idol. He did this by distinguishing between pure reason, which had no objective validity, and practical reason or what theologians called conscience or the moral faculty.

Here his temperament and environment counted effectively. Although he was a Prussian he had Scottish ancestry on one side and had been reared in a dour puritanical home. Probably he was impotent before he was 30. And in settling down to a study of his own rare type of moral consciousness he imagined that he was studying the moral sentiments of the race in general (of which he knew about as much as a virtuous nun does). He soon found that this practical or moral reason contained a "categorical imperative"; that is to say, it orders a man to be virtuous and rebukes certain actions, not because of consequences his act may have but absolutely. So all the attempts that had been made to found a utilitarian system of ethics, enforcing certain lines of conduct and forbidding others on social grounds, were wrong. In short the voice of conscience, or practical reason, was the voice of God; and as a sanction was clearly needed for this categorical law, man must be an immortal being who will get his reward or punishment beyond the grave, as he so often does not get it now.

HEGEL

This sophistry began the fall of the authority of Kant, and the philosophers had to try again. Passing over two—Schelling (a Pantheist) and Fichte—who are now rarely mentioned, the prophet who really inherited the mantle of Kant was Hegel. His name is familiar as one of the little ironies of this philosophical world, although he was a drastic conservative in politics and most emphatically anti-Materialist (he did not admit the existence of matter). The Bolsheviks have borrowed the terminology of his system in their Dialectical Materialism. I need not attempt to describe it. Masson said, when Hegel's chief book was translated into English, that it was like introducing an elephant on some Pacific Island where the inhabitants would not know which was the head and which the tail. It is enough to say here that Hegel got rid of all these difficulties about the relations of matter and mind by finding that mind alone exists and is in a process of eternal evolution. Strictly speaking, he said that the real and the ideal are the same thing, but that is just one way of putting it. He did not, of course, say, like Berkeley (or later, Eddington) that all exists in the mind of God. He just said that all existence is Mind or the Absolute (which Theists promptly called God).

SCHOPENHAUER

Then came Schopenhauer who, reacting upon the failure of all these intellectual schemes, declared that the fundamental reality is Will. An unconscious great force or power is working upward to the level of wisdom and civilization in the evolution of the cosmos, and it is encountering in man's perversity such stubborn opposition that it may all end in failure. Hence his pessimism. Bernard Shaw clings pathetically in our time to this last colossal piece of sophistry in which the long line of the philosophers ended in the last century.

IX. GREATER WRITERS OF THE 18th CENTURY

Literary men and historians continue to describe a number of thinkers of the 18th century as "the French philosophers" yet you will rarely find any reference to them in any manual of the history of philosophy. Chief amongst them, were Montesquieu, Buffon, Voltaire, Rousseau, D'Alembert, Diderot, Helvetius, and D'Holbach: all, says the philosopher, learned but too superficial to be called philosophers. Of their learning there is no question, for apart from their works, some of them classics in the history of law, science, or mathematics, they wrote the greatest encyclopedia of knowledge that had yet appeared. And to say that they were superficial does not recommend the study of philosophy to us.

We saw in the last chapter how the philosophers led their followers from one cloud to another cloud, and even when in the end a philosopher like Lotze tried to select and put together the best thoughts of each he left us almost nothing of permanent value. Whereas these French writers, to whom we must add Goethe in Germany, Adam Smith and Gibbon in England, and Franklin and Jefferson in America, were pioneers in the tremendous accumulation of knowledge in the next century and did grand service in shifting the heavy burden of tradition and authority which still oppressed the mind of the race. But they were all Freethinkers in both the broad and the narrow meaning of the word, so it would not be advisable to admit that they did more for the intellectual progress of the race than the "profound" thinkers did. Some of us prefer an accurate to a profound thinker: an expert scientist to a Maritain.

For obvious reasons I could quote more errors and absurdities than ever in this century. As education spread and books multiplied, and as the work of exposing and eradicating the monstrous volume of errors (protected by a persecuting authority) proceeded slowly, the field for the absurdity-hunter becomes far larger. Some idea of the extravagance of reactionary writers will be given in the next chapter but here I must select only the greatest of the thousands of writers. I am not selecting these because they were all skeptics—three of the above were Atheists, two might be called Agnostics (the name was then simply skeptics), one a Pantheist, and four definite Deists—but taking them at their valuation in history; and it is a fact to be noted that the dozen ablest writers of the century were already Freethinkers. If you add a dozen distinguished writers of second rank—Condorcet, Turgot, Laplace (an Atheist until his work was over), Lessing, etc.—the skeptical element is still predominant.

Of course, they all made mistakes. Montesquieu, whose "Spirit of the Laws" is a classic in the history of law and democracy, made mistakes in some of his historical statements, which had not yet been checked and exposed. Voltaire, though a close student of the imperfect science of his time, made a number of blunders in physics and thought that the fossil shells discovered on the French and Swiss mountains had been dropped by the pilgrims who for centuries had passed on their way to Italy. Hume, we saw, blundered because he was tempted into the field of philosophy as well as history. Adam Smith, the founder of political economy, certainly did not strike the full economic truth at the first shot. Laplace's first serious attempt to work out, mathematically, a nebular theory of the origin of the solar system is entirely abandoned as impossible. I have neither the mind nor the space to examine minutely the work of these dozen great men, and those who know their high service will not scrutinize their works closely for something at which we may smile. But, to keep the proportion of this book, we will examine some of the errors of a few of them.

BUFFON

Buffon (1707-88) wrote a "Natural History" in 44 volumes which astonished and deeply impressed all Europe. A sour critic of the time said, it is true, that the reason for its extraordinary popularity was that the fine ladies of France were now able to read all about the sex-life of animals in elegant and easily-understood language. The truth is that it was, for the age, a monumental scientific work and a fine piece of literature. But although many sentences ("The style is the man," "Genius is patience," "This animal [the rhinoceros] is wicked: it defends itself if you attack it") are still quoted as specimens of Buffon's style, it was known after his death that he had had a large number of collaborators and many of the best pages had been written by these. On the other hand, the main work of these men was to collect stories of animal life from the accounts of natives and travellers, as Aristotle had done, and thousands of these had never been checked. Buffon, in fact, checked some of his own errors as he grew older. His great work was intended to be a summary of knowledge and it began with a theory of the origin of the earth. At first he had attributed all the rocks to the action of water but later he realized that the earth must at first have been incandescent and that it still has a high temperature in the interior.

I have said that Voltaire explained fossil shells as shed by pilgrims, which is an absurdity, but Buffon, though nearer to the study of these things, adopted a more absurd theory. Following a medieval idea instead of taking up that of Leonardo da Vinci, he said that these stones called fossils were just natural coagulations of matter in the rocks. On many points he ignored or rejected new discoveries, especially if they contradicted his own opinion, and often, as experts point out, merely because they had been made by his rivals. Instead of developing Descartes' idea that all life (except mental) is purely mechanical, he said:

"The forces which animate the animal are peculiar to it. It wills, acts, and determines itself."

Vitality, he said, is in each molecule of the body, and there is an infinite number of these vitalized molecules in the universe. The spermatozoa, on the other hand, which had recently been discovered, he would not admit to be alive. They were like "vinegar eels," etc.: just aggregations of the vital molecules which were shed by animal bodies, especially from their sex-organs. Many kinds of animals were in this way born by spontaneous generation. He had, on the other hand, the beginning of an idea of evolution. The jackal, wolf, and fox derived, he said, from a common ancestor; the horse had come from the zebra. He had only dim and partial glimpses of the truth, but he did emphatically oppose the teaching which was so useful to Bible-scholars, of Linnaeus, that species are fixed by the creator; he maintained that a species may change with the climate. But wherever religion seemed to be affected he was very cautious. Throughout he speaks of "the Creator" but he said later to a friend, Herault de Sechelles, who tells us this:

"I have everywhere mentioned the Creator, but you have only to omit the word and put in its place the power of nature."

Like so many distinguished men of the time who are classed as Deists, he seems to have had a more radical Skepticism.

D'ALEMBERT

Even the great mathematician D'Alembert, close friend of Diderot, seems to have been far from candid when religion was involved in his statements and would have welcomed the title Agnostic if it had then been invented. He said to Diderot, "I am tempted to think that all that we see is just a phenomenon with nothing outside ourselves." He had apparently heard of Hume's philosophy. At other times he would ask: "Why does anything exist?" Once Diderot said to him:

"You're dogmatically for a thing in the morning and dogmatically against it in the afternoon."

"Yes," said D'Alembert, "and in the evening I believe neither."

It is not an impossible frame of mind in a great mathematician who looks out from his world of abstractions—so few of them do—upon the world of seething political and religious problems and contradictions, but it is also a well known form of escapism.

The hesitation—hesitation either to decide or to tell his decision —runs all through his work and is in sharp contrast to the clearness and precision of his mathematical work. He hesitates to accept Descarte's claim that life is mechanical, but admits that he cannot see how the immaterial can act upon the material. He sees that "morality is a consequence of the establishment of societies," but he objects that "in certain circumstances the good of the individual does not coincide with the general good." He thinks that "freedom of will must be admitted in any system of morals for if man is not free all ideas of evil will be reduced to physical evil"—a clumsy expression for a mathematician—yet he sees the difficulty of admitting such freedom. He startles and annoys his colleagues by claiming that "the ecclesiastics of Geneva are at the bottom Deists: they are more than tolerant." In short, he was clearly an Atheist with so much concern about the high academic and social position he had won—he was a bastard and had spent his youth in poverty—that the paradox of his words is often not what he had in his own mind. But we must remember also that he had devoted himself above all to mathematics and mechanics. France owes him a great debt for the considerable extent to which he did identify himself with the dreaded Encyclopedists.

DIDEROT

Denis Diderot (1713-84), with whom he had a remarkable friendship, was in a different position. He was the son of a workingman, and the studies of his youth and even later were pursued in poverty and sacrifice. It was his monumental learning and high character that won for him the association of academic notabilities like Buffon and D'Alembert or rich men like Helvetius and d'Holbach. He was at first a Deist with a profound admiration for the English Deist Shaftesbury, but he transferred his admiration to Bayle and abandoned all religious beliefs. Like D'Alembert, he disliked the name Atheist, but he made no secret of his absolute Skepticism; and his "Letters of the Blind" was condemned to be burned by the common executioner. He was the chief writer and dominating spirit of the Encyclopedia, and it will be taken for granted that he repeated large numbers of the errors that still lingered in science and history. A French medical writer, Dr. S. Doublet, has recently issued a work ("Medicine in the Works of Diderot") which, while entirely sympathetic, shows this. Diderot made a serious study of anatomy, physiology, medicine, and natural history—it is only a theologian or a philosopher that can call these encyclopedists' superficial—and he was the first to point out that life is a function of the tissues of the body, and he was much firmer and clearer than Buffon in advocating evolution. But he, naturally, in most matters of detail followed the fashion in medieval science. He laid great stress on "humors" and their actions. In some patients, he said—and he had spent weeks in the hospitals of Paris—the humors have "the voracity of animals, the causticity of fire." We must be careful not to "drive them back into the blood" as this is apt to cause fever. He advocated bleeding, and was

57

often bled, but hemorrhage and diarrhea are, he said, the natural means of getting rid of humors. "Most diseases, if not all, are nervous," he said, and "every organ may be taken as a separate animal, as it has its own poison, its miasma." He believed that such diseases as scurvy, scrofula, and gout were hereditary, and that thunder aggravates diseases.

BENJAMIN FRANKLIN

These are inherited absurdities and count for little in the record of the great figures of the 18th century who beat a broad path for the scientific advance of the 19th. And it is the same with the two Americans, Franklin and Jefferson, whom all will admit to have been intellectually the greatest of their age and inferior to none in character. Adams said of Franklin that in his time he had a greater repute than Frederick the Great or Voltaire. That is, perhaps, an 18th century American view, but his epoch-making discoveries in electricity alone made him famous throughout Europe as well as America. He had a genius for scientific inquiry, though his diplomatic and political career allowed him only a few years for concentrated research, and he was—though he read Latin, French, Italian, and Spanish—so little acquainted with what literature already existed that he sometimes did not know whether he had made a discovery or not. Most Americans today know only, apart from his share in public affairs, that by experimenting with kites he proved that lightning was an electrical phenomenon—in the elegant Latin epitaph of Turgot, "He stole the thunder from the heavens and the scepter from the hands of tyrants"—but modern experts hold that in linking together the various manifestations of the electric "fluid" he "made a vital contribution to the general structure of electrical theory."

In a writer of such shrewd and solid judgment, convinced by his own research that the tradition of the ages had brought down a mass of ancient errors, we do not expect to find many illusions. On a superficial reading, these are mostly connected with religion. He remained a Deist to the end, believing in a future life and spoke so respectfully of Christ and Christianity that today it is not uncommon for religious writers to claim that he was orthodox. "As to Jesus of Nazareth, I think his system of morals and his religion, as he left them to us, the best the world ever saw or is likely to see," he wrote. But he elsewhere admits that he had doubts about the divinity of Christ—he clearly did not believe it—and considers that the version of his teaching now treasured in the churches is a corruption. How he knows that the original version was so sublime he never tells us. In his later years he whimsically said:

"It is a question I do not dogmatize upon, having never studied it, and I think it needless to busy myself with it now when I expect soon to have an opportunity of knowing the truth with less trouble."

Meantime, he added, "I see no harm in its being believed." It is the usual story of a social pressure that deprives his small religious creed of any value. While he was a man of fine character his sex-ideas were not at all the same as those which he called the wonderful teaching of Jesus. He had several natural children, and in France the widow of Helvetius was one of his mistresses. Those who feel confident that they would have stood out for martyrdom if they had lived in the 18th century may cast the first stone. Franklin was, both socially and scientifically, one of the grand figures of the age who led America to its true destiny.

THOMAS JEFFERSON

We should say the same of Jefferson, though in the matter of religion there was a more curious inconsistency. In Foley's "Jeffersonian Cyclopedia" the critical reader will note the poverty of the quotations under such headings as Jesus, Christ, Christianity, Churches, Immortality, Heaven, etc., but the compiler has dug out a large number of references to the Deity that would adorn the lips or the pen of an archbishop. In a letter of the year 1809, when he was over 60, we read:

"We devoutly implore assistance of Almighty God to conduct us happily through the great conflict."

There are two pages of this stuff. Yet, if you turn to the heading "Materialism," you find that Jefferson was as scornful of the idea of spirit as Zeno and most of the Greek phlosophers had been. I showed this from his correspondence with Adams years ago in my Little Blue Book "Seven Infidel Presidents," but the joke here is that in this careful Jeffersonian Cyclopedia there are quotations from the same letters which plainly express his dogmatic Materialism. For instance:

"To talk of *immaterial* existences is to talk of *nothings*. To say that the human soul, angels, or God are immaterial is to say they are nothings or that there is no God, no angels, no souls."

Compare with this his remarks on transmigration in a letter to a clergyman:

"It is not for me to pronounce on the hypothesis you present of a transmigration of souls from one body to another in certain cases. The laws of nature have withheld from us the means of physical knowledge of the country of spirits, and revelation has, for reasons unknown to us, chosen to leave us in the dark."

One suspects here a slight flavor of irony, but the innumerable references to God, the Creator of the Universe, cannot possibly be explained in that manner. Of what nature was this God of his if it was as material as Jupiter or Aphrodite? It is impossible to read his words in that sense nor can we think Jefferson guilty of so many years of insincerity. The only solution seems to be, difficult as it is, that Jefferson was an ordinary Deist until he ceased to be President and retired from public life in 1808 and then, in his mature years, became a dogmatic Materialist and therefore Atheist. To settle this point it would require a more extensive study of his letters and writings than I can find room for here, but it would be a matter of considerable interest to modern Americans if we could prove that one of the greatest of their countrymen became an Atheist as soon as release from the labors of office gave him leisure to study religion. It is enough for me here to point out the paradox.

In other matters connected with religion we find him retailing uncritically the conventions of his age:

"There never was a more pure and sublime system of morality delivered to man than is to be found in the four Evangelists . . . We all agree in the obligation of the moral precepts of Jesus, and nowhere will they be found delivered in greater purity than in his discourses.

"I sincerely believe in the general existence of a moral instinct. I think it the brightest gem with which the human character is studded and the want of it as more degrading than the most hideous of bodily deformities. I believe that the moral sense is as much a part of our constitution as that of feeling, seeing, or hearing; as a wise Creator must have seen to be necessary in an animal destined to live in society . . . Egoism in a broader sense has been presented as the source of moral action . . . So Helvetius, one of the best men on earth. But it is one step short of the ultimate question."

Here we have the two phases or facets of Jefferson's mind in one passage: the high praise of Helvetius, an Atheist and Materialist, and a religious and intuitional idea of the social code of conduct. I just state the paradox and leave the solution to some future student. But there were other matters in which Jefferson idly adopted the reactionary ideas of his time. In regard to women he was as old-fashinned as Washington:

"Our good ladies, I trust, have been too wise to wrinkle their foreheads with politics. They are content to soothe and calm the minds of their husbands returning ruffled from political debate."

We will not forget that on other great social questions, such as slavery, he was, especially for a southerner, miles ahead of his generation. Unequal thinking was inevitable in what was still a raw new civilization separated by 3,000 miles of ocean from France and Britain. Jefferson, for instance, failed remarkably to foresee the near future of America when he advocated that it should restrict itself to agricultural production and leave manufacture to the Old World:

"While we have land to labor let us never wish to see our citizens occupied at a work-bench or twisting a distaff . . . for the general operations of manufacture let our workshops remain in England."

How in matters of science and history he repeated many errors that were still unquestioned in his time I need not show. We prefer to remember the power and sanity of intellect with which Jefferson conceived new ideals that were to put an end to man's feudal stage.

GIBBON

Goethe in Germany and Gibbon in England might be taken as the remaining great minds and guides of the 18th century, and research would not fail to find absurdities in the large body of their writings and letters. Of Gibbon I need say little as he is identified with one great historical work, "The Decline and Fall of the Roman Empire," and in this magnificent pioneer work of the new history there were bound to be plenty of errors. For instance, he endorses the Christian fable that the great library of Alexandria was burned by the Arabs, whereas not only are the details of the story he accepts obviously legendary but the authority is late and worthless. Even in the famous two chapters in which he speculates on the rise of Christianity he commits serious errors; and, although these chapters have been bitterly attacked by theologians for a century, his mistakes are not of advantage to Skepticism but to Christianity. It is today the general opinion of historians that accuracy—faithfulness to the imperfect material then available—is one of the chief characteristics of his work, but, as the notes in Bury's edition show, the accepted authorities led him into many unimportant errors.

GOETHE

The genius of Goethe roamed over nearly every field of culture and it is not difficult to convict him of error and even absurdity. In science, for instance, while he more or less discovered the Glacial Period in geology and welcomed and to some extent developed the theory of evolution, he was bound to be unlucky in the course of his original speculations. Most notable of these was his theory of color. His stay in a colony of artists roused his curiosity about color, and he believed that by his own experiments he proved that Newton's theory of color was wrong. He once said to Eckermann:

"I attach no importance to all that I have done as a poet but I do claim superiority in that I was the only man of my age to learn the true nature of color."

But his theory was, from the scientific angle, crude and leagues astray. He held that white light is simple, not compound, and that colors are due to some sort of blend of light and darkness or the passage of light through different translucent media. At the other end of the scale we are not surprised to find that he never understood the French Revolution, though the second part of *"Faust"* and *"Wilhelm Meister"* show

how zealous he became for social justice and progress. He was a grand figure in a difficult age, and we do not smile if the pioneer opening up a new world loses his way now and again. That was the position of these great humanists of the 18th century.

X. LEADERS OF THE NAPOLEONIC AGE

At the beginning of the present century collections of the mistakes of scientific men enjoyed a wide popularity both in the religious and the philosophical world. They were, in part, an attempt to weaken the growing public confidence in science but partly the familiar retort, that seems to give satisfaction to many folk: "You made blunders as well as we did." But there is a considerable difference between the two kinds of blunders. The scientific investigator fully admits that he has to proceed in part by guesses or hypotheses or theories. He has to interpret what he observes and, like the good detective, whose method closely resembles his, he tries one interpretation of the clues after another until he finds one that is beyond doubt or challenge. But the mistake of the theologians since the days of Copernicus and Galileo, and of the philosophers during the earlier part of that period, was to reject plainly observed facts or solidly established interpretations of them in the name of the dogmatic authority of Moses or Aristotle; and this obstinacy drove them to accept the discredited blunders of a more ignorant age or to wrap themselves in contortions at which we have the right to smile.

In the Catholic world much of this continued to the 19th century even in regard to the Copernican theory, as the Vatican, with its usual stubbornness, if not ignorance, maintained its opposition until the 19th century, when it was still forbidden in Catholic colleges to teach that the sun is the center of the solar system. In the 18th century a prominent English writer wrote a scornful refutation of the theory. "How," he asks, "can any man walk 200 yards to any spot if the moving superficies of the earth does carry it from him?" As late as the 30's of the 19th century we find Newman (later Cardinal) saying in a sermon delivered in Oxford University:

"Scripture says that the sun moves and the earth is stationary and science that the earth moves and the sun is comparatively at rest. How can we determine which of these opposite statements is the very truth till we know what motion is?"

Others, and not only Catholics, maintained the old idea that the earth was a level platform not a globe. As late as 1857 a book was published in London with the title "The Earth Not a Globe," and one of the leading provincial papers said that it "would seem to invalidate some of the most important conclusions of modern astronomy." One of the arguments was that navigators always use plot maps, not globes! Although astronomy was now making rapid progress and using giant telescopes monstrous ideas found publication. In 1863 a man named Hailes, publishing a freak system, offered to bet $500,000 to $5,000 that he could prove that "the sun is a crystalline body receiving the radiance of God." We should have the same effect, he said, "if the sun should be removed and a terrestrial body of ice placed in its stead."

The flat-earth theory was soon yielded by religious folk generally. When navigators began to sail to South Africa, South America, Australia, and New Zealand—round the earth, in fact—divines discovered that the Bible does not expressly say, however much it may imply, that the earth is not a globe. But almost every advance in astronomy was resisted. Giant telescopes came into use early in the 19th century, and it was discovered that many stars were double or multiple. On this announcement one of the most select publications of the Church of England observed;

"We have forgotten the name of the Siderophil who lately discovered that the fixed stars are not single stars, but appear in the heavens, like soles in the market, in pairs. While a second astronomer, under the influence of that competition in trade which the political economists tell us is so advantageous to the public, professes to show us, through his superior telescope, that apparently single stars are really three. Before such wondrous mandarins of science how continually must homunculi like ourselves keep in the back-ground."

Sixty or 70 years ago this contempt of science was still as common all over America and Europe as the scorn of Communism is today. The Methodist head of the Vanderbilt University said at a Conference of his church in 1878:

"This is an age in which scientific authority, having divested itself of the habiliments that most adorn and dignify humanity, walks abroad in shameless denudation."

One could quote reams of that sort of denunciation of the devilry of science until near the end of the last century. Then it became a respectable conflict of science and religion. Today religious readers are assured that there never was a conflict of science and religion. Half-informed camp-followers of science like McCabe prowled about in No Man's Land potting stray and misguided theologians.

As far as astronomy is concerned divines generally now discovered that "the heavens proclaim the glory of God" and astronomy just supplies us with spectacles to see it more clearly. It is amusing to read how the reluctance to yield before the advance of science was particularly stubborn in regard to comets. The ancient idea was, we saw, that they were exhalations of inflammable gas from pestilential marshes, and the medieval theologians had worked out that God set them on fire to warn and to punish men, as they "shook plague and murder from their hair." Even some of the great astronomers of the 16th century dared not attack this belief, but others did, and what we may call the War of the Comet lasted several centuries. When Halley's Comet appeared in 1682 a Fellow of the British Royal Society wrote in his diary, "Lord, fit us for whatever changes it may portend." At the time a Russian archbishop was on trial for some misdeed and, pointing to the heavens, he said to his judges: "God will sweep you all away!" Halley proved that comets had no connection with the earth, but the famous Dutch theologian, Professor Vossius, thundered: "The history of all times shows comets to be the messengers of misfortunes." The Catholic rector of a university at the time wrote:

"Comets are exhalations, hot and dry, fatty and well condensed, inflammable and kindled in the uppermost regions of the air . . . the fatty sticky material of a comet may be kindled from sparks falling from any heavenly bodies or by a thunder-bolt."

He had himself, he said, seen one graze the summit of Vesuvius, and Naples would have been destroyed if it had not been protected by the blood of St. Januarius. Some Protestant divines thought this too rationalistic. A German professor wrote that the comet is "the thick smoke of human sins rising every day, every hour, every moment, full of stench and horror, before the face of God and becoming gradually so thick as to form a comet, with curled or plaited tails, which at last is kindled by the hot and fiery anger of the Supreme Heavenly Judge." One of the most learned British bishops of the 17th century said that comets are "flying hells" in which the souls of the damned are tortured. A learned British professor of the 18th century said that it was with the tail of a comet that God broke the crust of the earth and caused the Flood. The Puritans of New England were, of course, fierce against the impious attempt to rob God of his red flags, but all over the world the old horror remained amongst the ignorant. In fact, as late as 1818 the British *Gentleman's Magazine*, which would have shuddered at the charge of ignorance, said that the comet of that year killed all the flies and caused a woman to have four children at a birth. In 1910, I was in Australia when Halley's Comet re-appeared, and I found the New South Wales official astronomer, a pious gentleman, advising folk, through the press, to remain indoors when the comet was nearest to the earth.

Meantime the advance of geology led to another of those fierce skirmishes which preceded the general battle. The Arabs and Persians had opened the avenue of geological exploration, and possibly Leonardo da Vinci had got, indirectly, from them the idea, so eccentric and so dangerous in his time, that fossils are the petrified remains of ancient animals and plants. Palissy followed Da Vinci but the idea was still so startling in the 18th century that Voltaire would not admit it. He did not, however, attribute them, as the philosophers and theologians (following Aquinas) did, to a "lapidific force" or to malformations in the rocks. He knew only of fossil shells and suggested that these (high up on the Alps) had fallen from pilgrims' hats. But field geologists were now studying the strata and realizing that the earth had been gradually formed; and this harmonized with Da Vinci's theory of fossils. But it was a darker menace than ever to the faith. Hadn't God created the earth, the plants, the animals, and man just as they are, and only about 4,000 years ago? Archbishop Ussher is credited with the 4,000 years theory, but it had been worked out, and may be worked out from biblical data by any man, by a series of divines. It was, however, a far more learned British divine, Dr. Lightfoot, Vice-Chancellor or Cambridge University and reputed one of its most famous scholars, who discovered that the Trinity did this stupendous work—"created heaven and earth, center and circumference, in the same instant and with clouds full of water," at 9 a.m. of the 20th of October, 4004 B.C. And this was said by one of the ablest scholars of his church when science was fairly advanced.

From the end of the 17th century divines now smelt a double emanation of sulphur from the pit. One of the most learned bishops of the time, Burnet, countered with a "Sacred Theory of the Earth" which brought into harmony with the Bible these features of nature that geologists were misrepresenting. The earth was created with a smooth surface, perfect shape, a most graceful and happy population of living things. The lion lay down with the lamb and even the dog had no fleas. Then Adam sinned, and God soured the face of the earth. But again men became wicked and God had to strike once more. Underneath the shell or crust the earth had a mighty volume of water, and God "broke the foundations of the deep"—another great scholar, Whiston, said that he hit them with the tail of a comet—and out poured the waters that covered the entire earth. Naturally this drowned innumerable animals and made a hideous mess of what had been the land-surface of the earth, which it now carved into hills and valleys. Was there any wonder, Burnet asked, if you saw strata of the crust that had plainly been formed from beds of sediment often twisted out of shape, and containing masses of bones of animals at all levels? Twenty or 30 years later a Swiss theologian, Scheuchzer, brought out a book with the title "A Human Witness of the Deluge," which gave great joy, for it contained a drawing of a crushed and broken animal frame that had recently been unearthed—of a wicked man drowned in the Flood. It appears to have been a fossil giant salamander or reptile. Both books were translated into many languages, and their "sound scientific" teaching repeated by hundreds of religious writers and pamphleteers. Bones of dinosaurs and mammoths began to appear. These, of course, were the bones of the giants who lived before the Flood.

The idea was useful to theologians in many ways. For one thing it reconciled the evil and disorder of the world with the goodness of the Creator. It was all beautiful—something like the old Persian idea of the earth as Ahura Mazda created it, before Angra Mainyu got up to his dirty tricks—at first, but when men sinned so much God was, to his great grief, compelled to turn it into a Vale of Tears. There were, it is true, theologians who would not admit that even before the Flood the world had anything to be ashamed of. Everything was really good and providential. A Fellow of the British Royal Society, Dr. N. Grew, proved it (again from sound science). He said:

"A crane, which is scurvy meat, lays but two eggs in the year, but a pheasant and partridge, both excellent meat, lay and hatch 15 to 20 . . . If nettles sting it is to secure an excellent medicine for children and cattle . . . if the bramble hurts a man it makes all the better hedge, and if it chances to prick the owner it tears the thief. Weasels, kites, and other hurtful animals induce us to watchfulness, thistles and moles to good husbandry; lice oblige us to cleanliness in our bodies, spiders in our houses, and the moth in our clothes."

Reams of this stuff were written by pious and learned naturalists. One notices the hand of providence in the bug, as it is so apt to crawl on to your clean white collar and get caught. Others again took refuge in the ancient idea of spontaneous generation, which science still admitted. God had not specially created flies and fleas, spiders and scorpions, and so on. The Bible said that the earth "brought them forth," and Aristotle agreed with Moses. But the more congenial theory was that God made everything jolly, and "Sin" fully explained the spoiling of it all at the Flood. Granville Penn, another famous divine, said, against the geologists, that "our earth has undergone only two revolutions, the Creation and the Deluge." A British cleric, Dean Buckland, who did know geology, was called into the arena, but he was so much intimidated by the chorus of divines that a wag wrote:

Some doubts were once expressed about the Flood:
Buckland arose, and all was clear as mud.

Puerile as the idea of the Flood seems to us today—though it is given as Catholic doctrine in the Catholic Encyclopedia (1908) that there was a Flood and it destroyed the whole human race except Noah's boating party—the fury of the battle over it raged until after the middle of the last century. In 1860, a London publisher, Smith, well known for his dictionaries, encyclopedias, etc., announced a great Dictionary of the Bible. When the D part of it came out you were told at "Deluge" to look out for "Flood." When the F's came out you were referred to "Noah." The editors dare not pronounce. Ten years later we found the Assyrian tablets which showed that the story in Genesis is borrowed from an ancient Babylonian (or Sumerian) folk-story.

Meantime the battle had extended to other fields and brought out fresh floods of absurdity. One of the chief reasons for this tremendous zeal for the Flood was that on the lines of geological science the nature of the strata and the fossils opened up tremendous abysses of past time, but, as we saw, the beginning of the world was fixed at about 4000 B.C. Where was this challenge going to end? Already in 1794 Erasmus Darwin, grandfather of the more famous Charles, had claimed that man and all the animals were evolved, not created. The divines and their followers were more strident than ever. In 1802 the leading writer of France, Chateaubriand, insisted in his most famous work, "The Genius of Christianity," that God created the world 6,000 years ago just as it is today:

"It was part of the perfection and harmony of the nature that was unfolded before the eyes of men that the deserted nests of last year's birds should be seen in the trees, and that the seashore should be covered with shells which had been the abode of fish, and yet the world was quite new, and nests and shells had never been inhabited."

Another imaginative pietist suggested that the fossils were created as models of the animals—you would almost say broken toys of the deity. Gosse, a really distinguished British naturalist, wrote:

64

"Neither reason nor revelation will justify us in extending the origin of the natural system beyond 6,000 years from this day."

Rocks that show by ancient scratches that a glacier once flowed over them were no difficulty. God created them like that. When men of science talked like that you can faintly imagine what the preachers were saying. Clergy and gentry applauded the verse of the famous poet Cowper:

> Some drill and bore
> The solid earth, and from the strata there
> Extract and register by which we learn
> That he who made it and revealed its date
> To Moses lied.

All this went on for a quarter of a century after Sir Charles Lyell, the great geologist and one of England's foremost scientific men at the time, had put beyond question in his classic work, "The Principles of Geology," that the earth's crust had been gradually formed during ages. The geologists, in fact, demanded more time than the astronomers. In the early years of this century, the successors of the priests who had fought under the banner "Creation, 4004 B.C." were jeering at scientists of the last century who had said that the earth could be more than 100,000,000 years old. They omitted to mention that it was a religious scientist, Lord Kelvin, who said this, and they were, of course, entirely ignorant that the Atheist Buchner, whose book, "Force and Matter," had sold by the hundred thousand had, in 1855, given estimates of the age of the earth rising to 6,000 million years!

But the scientific army was advancing on all fronts and at every step it met a shower of jibes and absurdities. Archeologists found the remains of Stone and Metal Ages stretching over millennia before the dawn of civilization. "What," said an eminent Christian Egyptologist. "Why, Egypt laughs the idea of a rude Stone Age, a polished Stone Age, and Bronze Age, and an Iron Age, to scorn." The scientific powers drove on like slow tanks. Darwin brought out a scientific scheme of evolution. Those who followed him, said one of the leading reviews, were "under the frenzied inspiration of the inhalation of mephitic gas." The book (based upon evidence patiently collected during 20 years) was "a huge imposture from beginning to end," "a jungle of fanciful assumptions," etc. One of the most fashionable bishops of the Church of England, "Soapy Sam" Wilberforce, thought that he could afford to ridicule it in a scientific gathering at Oxford (the British "Home of Lost Causes") and you may have read Huxley's crushing retort:

> "If I had to choose I would prefer to be a descendent of a humble monkey rather than of a man who employs his knowledge and eloquence in misrepresenting those who are wearing out their lives in the search for truth."

The reviewer of Darwin's book in the *Times* said that it was "reckless and unscientific," an "utterly unsupported hypothesis." An American Methodist bishop annihilated it in a conference of his church. There were, he assured them of his own scientific knowledge, beds in the district with mingled remains of "the monk-rat, the ichthyosaurus, and the coprolite." He did not even know that coprolite means fossilized dung. A great preacher in Paris, Msgr. Segur, said:

> "These infamous doctrines have for their only support the most abject passions. Their father is pride, their mother impurity, their offspring revolutions. They come from hell and return thither, taking with them the gross creatures who blush not to proclaim and accept them."

As a description of the gentle Darwin and the puritan Huxley this is, as the French say, *impayable*. A learned French physician sent the Pope a copy of the work in which he completely demolished evolution;

but the howlers that the Pope perpetrated in his reply may be reserved for a later chapter. Don't forget that Catholics, as well as their spiritual brethren the Fundamentalists, still use this language about evolution and evolutionists. They still libel Haeckel as they once libelled Darwin.

XI. POISON GAS AGAINST SCIENCE

There was the same grand pyrotechnic display and outpour of poison gas all along the line of the scientific advance. Most Americans will have read what was said in the religious world when Franklin robbed Jupiter of his thunderbolts by showing that it was all just a matter of electricity. There was a big earthquake in South America just afterwards and preachers in Massachusetts assured their congregations that it was due to "those iron points invented by the sagacious Mr. Franklin." Few buildings were so frequently struck as church spires yet none were so reluctant to protect them with "the heretical rod" as the clergy. It was the same in all countries. In Germany the fact was published that 400 church towers had been struck in 33 years, but the Lutheran ministers were as bad as those of New England. The Catholics were, of course, the last to yield. The tower of St. Mark's cathedral in Venice was repeatedly struck before they would protect it. In another Venetian church the authorities had stored 200,000 pounds of gunpowder. In 1767 (17 years after Franklin's discovery) it still had no conductor. It was struck and the powder fired. The explosion destroyed, with great loss of life, one-sixth of the city.

Even in innocent natural history the bishops brandished their croziers against the advancing scientific demons. The row over biblical criticism and the infallibility of the Bible often turned on ancient petty superstitions that were accepted in the sacred book. One wag wrote:

> The bishops all had sworn to shed their blood
> To prove 'tis true the hare doth chew the cud.
> Oh, bishops, doctors, and divines beware.
> Weak is the faith that hangs upon a hair.

Dragons, basilisks, and other mythical creatures had to go, but if they were mentioned in the Old Testament it was like pulling teeth. Said a German professor:

> "Who would dare to deny the existence of the unicorn since Holy Scripture names him with distinct praises?"

Philology had been founded early in the last century, but stuffy old divines still held that the original language was Hebrew—in what other tongue could God have spoken to Adam in Paradise—and the Tower of Babel was the tragic theater in which the great diversity of languages began. As late as 1857 one of them wrote:

> "The Hebrew is the primary stock from which all languages are derived ... Sanscrit is a dialect of Hebrew, and the manuscripts found with mummies agree precisely with the Chinese version of the Psalms of David."

Comparative religion was replacing the old idea that all religions that were not Christian were either inspired by the devil or were hopelessly stupid. The dissection of their better points now led to the modern theological theory of a "progressive revelation" and a discovery of profound mystery and symbolism in the creeds of ancient Egypt. Godfrey Higgins, whose "Anacalypsis" made a great noise in the last century, wrote such rubbish as:

> "The Buddhists of Upper India, of whom the Phoenician Canaanite Melchisedech was a priest, who built the Pyramids, Stonehenge, Carnak, etc., will be shown to have founded all the

ancient mythologies of the world which, however varied and corrupted in ancient times, were originally one and proceeded on principles sublime, beautiful, and true."

The superstition that all the world lay in darkness and the shadow of death until the coming of Christ was, in the minds of those who still opposed science, giving place to a new group of absurdities: that God had revealed himself to the race from the beginning of history, that the seers of the old world were far wiser than the scientific men and philosophers of today, that the pyramids of Egypt embodied an advanced knowledge of astronomy as well as a lost art of engineering, that flea-bitten fragments of the half-civilized race like the Tibetans had a marvellous wisdom stored in their squalid monasteries, and so on.

The worst of it was that even in practical matters the lamentable biblical inheritance continued to block the lines of advance. None know better than Americans what appalling effect it had in the struggle for the abolition of slavery. It was a liberal divine who said that it would have been a good thing for the abolitionists if all the churches of America had dropped through the floor of the planet. Jesus and Paul had treated slavery as a normal and legitimate human institution. St. Augustine had explained that God had ordained it as one of the punishments of sin. Even the belief in witchcraft, with all the terrible suffering it had entailed during 800 years, was stoutly held by divines against the assaults in the 18th century of the great Freethinkers (Voltaire, Beccaria, etc.) The most deeply religious oracle in Europe, John Wesley, declared that "the giving up of witchcraft is in effect the giving up of the Bible." The action of devils was still seen everywhere. Until the end of the 18th century the insane were apt to be regarded as possessed by the devil, who was to be driven out by scourging and forcing filth into the patient as well as by prayer. The third edition of the Encyclopedia Britannica said, under the title of "Demoniacs": "The validity of demoniacal possession stands upon the same evidence with the Gospel system in general."

The success of medicine in reducing the terrible volume of pain and suffering that had lain upon the race for ages was thwarted by the pious. The Popes of the Middle Ages had hampered the progress of anatomy and fostered a most mischievous belief in the efficacy of shrines, relics, pilgrimages, and all kinds of profitable devices. The reformers had swept away this reliance upon miraculous cures, but Luther's morbid belief in the activity of devils had led to the retention of the other great superstition in the way of medical progress. Great advances like inoculation and the use of anesthetics were resisted as furiously as the installation of lightning-conductors. Vaccination was introduced in the 18th century, and one could quote a large number of clerical denunciations of it. Small-pox, the preacher cried, was "a judgment of God on the sins of the people" and to attempt to prevent it by inoculation was "an encroachment on the prerogative of Jehovah." Boston preachers raised the charge of murder against a local doctor who unsuccessfully vaccinated a patient. It was, one divine said, "an artificial way of depopulating a country."

It was about the middle of the last century when American dentists introduced the use of gas to lessen the pain which the race had endured for thousands of years in the removal of decayed teeth. Then the Scottish surgeon Simpson discovered the use of chloroform. Until then the operating room of a hospital "resembled a butcher's shambles" said a medical writer of the time:

"The patient was held down by three or four powerful arms as the surgeon boldly and rapidly did his work despite the screams, stopping, perhaps, only roughly to abuse the patient for some agonized movement which had interfered with his course of action. The poor wretch saw the instruments handled one by one."

And there was the usual cackle from the pulpit when surgeons wanted to mitigate this suffering. In Catholic Dublin the opposition was long sustained. It was particularly bitter against Simpson when he began to soften the pains of child-bearing. Here the Bible plainly said that as a punishment for her invasion of the reserved orchard Eve and all her female descendants to the end of time must bring forth children "in sorrow." Yes, said Simpson, who knew his Bible well, but the same Lord God "caused a deep sleep to fall upon Adam" when he prepared to take out one of his ribs and make a woman out of it. This was, of course, the devil quoting scripture. The violent opposition continued.

These are just a few specimens of the absurdities with which divines were driven in opposing the Bible to the discoveries of science. Even in social life old superstitions were either upheld or treated with tenderness. Most folk know how, until the later Middle Ages, the Church condemned the taking of any interest on a loan as a mortal sin. It is not generally known that Luther also called it theft, and that in spite of the immense development of business and banking in modern times, the Catholic Church still boggled. In 1830 the Vatican again refused to disown the old doctrine of "usury." In 1872 it replied that it was no sin to take even 8 percent of your capital. It had begun to seek the most profitable investments for its own capital.

By that time science was taking over every province of real life and there were few in which it did not encounter opposition from the clergy. But so many educated folk recognized that science meant truth sweeping old ignorance out of its path that a deeper rebellion arose in the religious world itself. What was called the Higher Criticism of the Bible, which drew another shower of theological expletives, was left almost entirely to consecrated writers. Scientists and Freethinkers generally just stood on the edge of the arena and smiled. They smiled more broadly than ever when, in the second half of the last century, there appeared an enormous and diverting literature that purported to reconcile the teaching of science with the teaching of the Bible. To the absurdities to which this zeal gave birth I will return later.

XII. THE NEW SOCIAL ORACLES

With the 19th century the river of books that flowed over the planet became broader and deeper. The population increased rapidly after the close of the Napoleonic Wars, and with the establishment of state systems of free schools in all leading countries the number of readers rose to millions. Yet for many reasons it is not difficult to restrict the number of the men I choose here to illustrate, for our encouragement, the blunders of great minds. The principal writers of general interest in the last century are still read and their opinions are widely known, while scientific writers of distinction no longer hold those beliefs about nature and its animal populations or about the structure of the universe which have chiefly entertained us throughout this volume. In fact, scientists now increasingly specialize and the opinions or errors of many who were esteemed intellectual giants in their time—Agassiz, Pasteur, Helmholtz, Ricardo, Faraday, Huxley, Darwin, Le Conte, Comte, Lester F. Ward, etc.—are not much discussed today outside the history of the science which each cultivated. I will therefore select here a few literary men of international influence who were regarded in most countries as social oracles.

For America it is obviously best to choose the leading writers of the Boston or Transcendentalist School. To the poets, political authors, historians, and scientists who make up a large part of the best American literature of the last century we do not look for the kind of blunders and eccentricities which interest us here, and the opinions of novelists are not taken seriously. The great social oracles, wielding a considerable influence until late in the century were Emerson and other New England writers who thought that they were making a new, permanent, and incalculably important contribution to man's thinking. We might, in fact, dismiss even these with the remark that the fundamental blunder of the whole group is expressed in the name, the Transcendentalists, which is often used as a common label of them. It means that in forming their creed they "transcended" experience and had their mental roots in a mystic world that was reached only by a sort of intuition. Splendid as their service was in breaking the tyranny over men's minds of the older New England religion, their creed is not for us moderns; and its very mysticism prevented them from applying moral principles too closely to the collective life. Like Confucius in ancient China, they aimed to make a man a "gentleman"—as the translations of the Chinese classics express the ideal Confucian man—and looked to him to apply his own refinement in the conduct of life. For the realistic workers and writers of the modern world, Emersonianism is as dead as Confucianism is in China.

RALPH WALDO EMERSON

Emerson, on account of the charm and purity of his style, is the chief representative of the group, and illustrates the fundamental blunder of these writers who used to be regarded as America's finest guides to conduct on the higher plane. In one of his most characteristic essays, "The Over-Soul," which shows in its very title how the old puritanism and a good deal of mysticism remained when they had exorcized the devil of the fierce old theology, he says:

"The argument which is always forthcoming to silence what we conceive to be extraordinary hopes of man, namely the appeal to experience, is for ever invalid and vain . . .

"Man is a stream whose source is hidden. Always our being is descending into us from we know not whence. I am constrained every moment to acknowledge a higher origin for events than the will I call mine. As with events, so is it with thoughts. When I watch that flowing river which out of regions I see not pours for a season its streams into me, I see that I am a pensioner: not a cause but a surprised spectator of this ethereal water, that I desire and look up and put myself in the attitude of reception; that from some alien energy the visions come . . . that Unity, that Over-Soul, within which every man's particular being is contained and made one with all others; that common heart of sincere conversation is the worship to which all right action is submissive: that overpowering reality which compels our tricks and talents . . . the Eternal One . . . the Highest Law.

"We lie open on one side to the deeps of spiritual nature, to all the attributes of God. Justice we see and know: Love, Freedom, Power. These natures no man ever got above, but always they tower over us, and most in the moment when our interests tempt us to renounce them.

"If a man wants to know when the Great God speaketh he must "go into his closet and shut the door," as Jesus said. He must listen to himself, withdrawing himself from all the accents of other men's devotions . . . He that finds God a sweet enveloping thought to him never courts other company. When I sit in that presence who shall overcome me?"

In "English Traits" he says:

"If religion be the doing of all good and for its sake the suffering of all evil, that divine secret has existed in England from the days of Alfred to those of Romilly, of Clarkson, and of Florence Nightingale."

I add this quotation only to show how this mysticism warps the judgment. It is a complete misconception of the character of the Middle Ages, a credulous acceptance of the Catholic version, because this suited

Emerson's disposition; and the greater English figures of Emerson's own time were not Romilly—good man as he was—and certainly not Clarkson, but Owen, Bentham, Place, and Mill. But they were Atheists and made Emerson shudder. W. D. Howells, who knew, and to a great extent followed, Emerson gives in his "Literary Friends and Acquaintances" a description of him that almost alienates an admirer. He had "an extraordinary indifference and coldness to men" and he forgot events as soon as they had happened. He speaks of his "Quaker calm" and "frosty Puritanism." He thought that "the habit of plain speaking had to be zealously guarded to keep it from becoming rude speaking." He closely followed the literary movement in America but, says Howells, "I doubt if he so fully appreciated the importance of the social movement." He agreed with the anti-slavery agitation but he "had no sympathy with those who think that the man who may any moment be out of work is industrially a slave." He even gives instances of pettiness of character in Emerson's personal conduct. Howells, who gives it as a general feature of these New England moralists that they declined to apply their beautiful regard for justice to the social and industrial order, is not altogether just to Emerson. In his fine essay "Man the Reformer," which is a lecture delivered to an audience of workers in 1841, Emerson shows that he was by no means indifferent to the social struggle. A typical sentence is:

> "What is man born for but to be a Reformer, a re-maker of what man has made, a renouncer of lies, a restorer of truth and good, imitating that great nature which embosoms us all, and which sleeps no moment on our old past but every hour repairs herself yielding us every morning a new day, and with every pulsation a new life?"

He was far from the temperament of an active reformer, but he knew that his ideal commanded reform.

Curiously enough, the reproach seems to have more ground when it is applied to the more practical Oliver Wendell Holmes. Not only did he, like all the others, resent any criticism of the established creeds, but he "sat in the seat of the scorner as far as Reform is concerned." He looked at the common folk "through the palings and over the broken bottles on the wall." Lowell was nearer to helping radicalism but lost all his zeal in his later years when "he had no faith in insubordination as a means of grace." Law and Order became his idols. Longfellow, who broadly belongs to the school, was much the same. They were all skeptics yet it is only from the gossipy pages of Howells' book that you learn that they did not believe in a personal God and personal immortality. It does not say much for the new Platonist idealism that it left men isolated in their own graceful comfort and indifferent to so many lies and injustices. Indeed, in transferring the moral ideal from its Christian frame to the clouds, instead and finding a basis for it in social needs, they created a new superstition which still has an evil influence as surely as did Aristotle when he invented metaphysics.

ABRAHAM LINCOLN

If we care to do so we can find much of a different kind to censure in Abraham Lincoln. It is well known how once, in mature manhood, when his son was bitten by a dog he took him miles away to be cured by a "madstone." Hapgood shows that "to the very day of his death Lincoln never failed to believe in supernatural portents," and that "superstition, faith, and doubt were inextricably mixed up in him." It was not from political expediency only that he kept his views about religion so veiled that Christian writers still claim him. As to the other great American oracle of the last century, Walt Whitman, we hardly look to him for opinions. His fiery gospel of brotherhood did so much service that we will not quarrel with his claim that it had a mystic or "religious" basis.

70

THOMAS CARLYLE

It is more interesting to study the famous British counterpart of Emerson, Thomas Carlyle: I mean counterpart in the sense that he rejected orthodoxy, based his fiery moral idealism on a mystic or Pantheistic conception of the universe, and by his masterly style of writing won an immense influence in the whole English-speaking world and even beyond it. But even more clearly than any of the American transcendentalists he betrayed the weakness of this attempt to find a basis for his moral idealism that should be neither Christian nor, as he would scornfully say, utilitarian. The New Englanders were generally indifferent to the humanitarian plans of the new age. Carlyle bitterly opposed most of them. While he denounced masters for exploiting the workers, he, on the other hand, contemptuously, and in his later years incessantly, attacked the reform movement as "patent-treacle philanthropy." A few quotations will suffice. On the long-overdue demand for prison reform he wrote (in the essay "Model Prisons," 1850):

"Most sick am I, O friends, of this sugary, disastrous jargon of philanthropy, the reign of love, the new era of universal brotherhood; and not Paradise to the Well-deserving but Paradise to all and sundry, which possesses the benighted minds of men and women in our day. Brotherhood! No, be the thought far from us. Poor old Genius of Reform, bedrid this long while; with little broken ballot boxes and tattered stripes of Benthamite Constitutions lying round him . . . Christian religion! Does the Christian or any other religion prescribe love of scoundrels?"

He bitterly attacks the prison-reformer Howard, who now has so honorable a place in the record of 19th-century reform, and maintains that crime is an incurable disease:

"My clear opinion is that we had better quit the Scoundrel province of Reform; better close that under hatches, in some rapid summary manner, and go elsewhere with our reform efforts . . . My sublime benevolent friends, don't you perceive, for one thing, that here is a shockingly unfruitful investment for your capital of Benevolence? If I had a commonwealth to reform or to govern, certainly it should not be the Devil's regiments of the Line that I would first concentrate all my attention on . . . Mark it, my diabolic friends, I mean to lay leather on the backs of you, collars round the necks of you . . . ye diabolic canaille."

The abolitionist movement was then sending its echoes across the Atlantic, especially as there were still slaves in the West Indies. In another essay, "The Nigger Question," Carlyle condemned the movement root and branch:

"Our grand proposed Association of Associations, the Universal Abolition-of-Pain Association, which is meant to be the consummate golden flood and summary of modern Philanthropies all in one, do *not* issue as a universal Sluggard and Scoundrel Protection Society . . .
"I never thought the rights of Negroes worth much discussing, nor the rights of man in any form; the grand point, as I once said, is the *mights* of man . . . All this talk of perfect equality, of black peasantry, and the other melancholy stuff that has followed from it, will first of all require to be undone."

Carlyle as an historian was supposed to know a good deal about the Middle Ages yet he advocates the revival of serfdom and compulsory labor:

"If the English cannot find the manner to make West Indian

71

blacks work they may rest assured there will another come (Brother Jonathan or still another) who can. He it is whom the gods will bid continue in the West Indies, bidding us ignominiously 'Depart, ye quack-ridden incompetents.' "

Not less sardonically he fell upon the idea of democracy, the extension of the franchise to the workers and the adoption of secret ballots at elections. In the essay "Parliaments" (1850) he says:

"By this time it is sufficiently apparent that the present Editor is not one of those who expect to see the country saved by further reforming the Reform Parliament [which gave the vote to the middle class] we have got . . . As to universal suffrage, can it be proved that since the beginning of the world there was ever given a universal vote in favor of the worthiest man or thing? . . . I will consult it about the quality of New Orleans pork, but as to the character of men I will ask it no question. There are such things as multitudes all full of beer and nonsense, even of insincere fictitious nonsense who by hypothesis cannot go wrong. What safety will there be in a thousand of the low brawling potwallopers and blockheads, of any rank whatever, if the Fact, namely the whole universe and the Eternal Destinies, be against me?"

Not democracy but aristocracy, the leadership of great men, is the political ideal, and he wrote some of his best books on despotic "heroes" of history. Even his history was false, under the influence of his ideal, for modern history recognizes that many of his model men were just medieval swashbucklers, often of corrupt or cruel character. In "Great Men" he writes:

"When, across the hundredfold poor skepticisms and constitutions . . . you catch sight of a William the Conqueror, a Tancred of Hauteville, and such like, do you not discern veritably some rude outline of a true God-made king? . . . Oh, Windbag, my right honorable friend, in very truth I pity thee. I say low or loud votings of thy poor fellow blockheads, of any kind, will never guide thee in any enterprise at all. Thou can'st not make a pair of shoes, sell a pennyworth of tape, or aught else."

It was the decade succeeding the Irish famine, and the "Irish Question" was agitating British minds for the first time. Carlyle referred to it as "our own white or sallow Ireland, sluttishly starving from age to age." The treatment of paupers, mainly worn-out workers, was another living issue. Carlyle was as sour as ever about schemes to care for them.

The interest of all this for us today is that Emerson and Carlyle and their followers were urging the world to cling to "spiritual realities" and "eternal moral verities" if it felt obliged to give up Christianity. They were scornfully opposed to Materialism, which would lower men's ideals, to science (the force that would presently enable men to carry out their philanthropies), and particularly to the new evolutionary science ("a gospel of dirt," Carlyle spat at it). But it is upon the work of the Materialist-Atheist humanitarians, against whom they warned the world—Bentham, Owen, Place, Grote, Mill, etc.—that their nation went on in the last part of the century to build up a greater civilization than ever. But let us examine a few more spiritual oracles before we draw the final lesson; for in this chapter at least the aberrations of great minds have a living interest for us today.

MAZZINI

Another oracle who had great influence in Europe was Mazzini. He was a definite Theist and made a profession of being a Christian, without church or dogmas, but he is of interest here because he was a violent anti-Materialist and a most eloquent spouter for spiritual realities. He fell into quarrels with Garibaldi because he (the finest

Italian liberator) was an Atheist—and despised Mazzini's mysticism—and with his best British supporter Holyoake because he was a Secularist. But I need not quote. We respect the sacrifices that Mazzini made for the liberation of Italy from the Pope and the feudal monarchs, but there his idealism ended. His vague rhetoric about the brotherhood of man did not move even himself to enter into the social, political, and scientific advances of his time. "Spiritual realities" again proved sterile. And this was still clearer in the case of the Russian ascetic, Tolstoi. He had for some years an amazing influence but in so far as it was useful it was almost confined to peace propaganda. This might have sufficed to leave us in debt to him, but unfortunately he rendered a considerable disservice with his asceticism; again an outcome of his "spiritual realities." The sanest hope of the 19th century was that science would enable the race to create such wealth that it could carry out all its dreams of social betterment and give the individual a richer life. Tolstoi advocated a poorer life and so was indifferent to the broader ideals of his time. Science was gradually giving men a conception of life that would, or will, sweep away all the mischievous old creeds. Tolstoi used all his art to discredit science as a guide and left his few genuine followers groping for an imaginary "meaning of life."

NIETZSCHE

Different, but still a blunderer from his opposition to science and Materialism, was the great German prophet Nietzsche. We so much appreciate Nietzsche's splendid work in shaking the contemporary mind from its slavery to conventions and traditions, while we recognize that as a fiery ironic poet he said much that was just paradox or exaggeration, that we do not examine him as critically as we do Tolstoi. You can cut out of his work such horrid--sounding phrases as, "A just war hallows every cause," or, "If you're going to the women don't forget the whip," but a man must be ignorant of his character to imagine that he ever condemned military callousness, cruelty, or injustice. Yet he made serious blunders. He made almost as fierce attacks as Carlyle on modern humanitarianism or philanthropy and he was totally false in his history when he found the origin of this in Christianity. He attacked the new doctrine of evolution, which not only brought a basic conception of life but a direct encouragement to work for its betterment. His exaggerated emphasis on individualism encouraged the blinder opposition to Socialism, and even what may be called his chief gospel, the transvaluation of values, was confused. It finally delivered man from bondage to the conventional or the Christian code, but it put undue emphasis on strength and the Dionysiac urge and obscured the sound social basis of ideals of conduct.

KARL MARX

Of the second, and possibly greater, German prophet of the century as measured by world-influence, Karl Marx, it is not necessary to say much. Distinguished Socialist writers have strongly criticized his theory of surplus value and claimed that it is just another name for the familiar profit of the capitalist, but we cannot blame Marx because features of his system which were natural in the political and economic world of his time are obstinately retained by many of his followers.

IBSEN

The great Scandinavian oracle Ibsen is, on the other hand, as much open to criticism, in a different way, as Nietzsche. He, too, rendered a magnificent service in disturbing the complacency and servility of the mind of his time but his work is apt to leave us depressed and uncertain. I detest the namby-pamby folk who bleat that destruction is an inferior thing and we must always be constructive. The great destroyers—Voltaire, Shelley, Ibsen, Schopenhauer, Nietzsche, etc.—have done splendid work for us. But a constructive plan of the new world, which was vitally necessary, was taking shape in the last century, and Ibsen's dramas did not encourage men to work confidently in it. Only a week ago I heard a condensed rendering of "Rosmersholm." It must have left undisciplined, especially artistic minds blank or vaguely dejected. Ibsen's friend and rival Bjornson, though lower in ability, was far sounder in his ideas.

HERBERT SPENCER

We must still talk of blunders when we turn to a third group of writers of high ability and great influence, in America and Britain, who though they dropped the mischievous emphasis on spiritual realities and made it plain that they meant only culture and idealism, not gods, angels, and souls, yet encouraged the contempt of Materialism. We may broadly call them the Agnostic school: Spencer, Huxley, Ward, etc. Herbert Spencer's most characteristic idea was that we must retain religion as an emotional attitude to a great Unknown and Unknowable underlying all that we perceive to exist. Ever since the time of Kant this word "underlie" has been worn to death and it is time it was buried. Science has sufficiently advanced to let us see that if there is an Unknown (and at present) Unknowable it is the obscure material—or energy, if you prefer—which curdles into electrons, protons, etc., and ripples in waves of different lengths. There is no more reason to take off our hats to it than to the Rockies. Huxley, as is well known, coined the word Agnostic for this anti-Materialist school. His admirers still dispute what he meant. In one place he explains, on the basis of Hume's philosophy, that we cannot know anything about anything that lies beyond (or "under," of course) objects perceived by our senses. That ancient absurdity was clearly a subterfuge. On other pages he says that, coming together in a club with a large number of other able men, each of whom had a positive knowledge about God—theistic or atheistic—he could only distinguish himself by saying that he had no knowledge or was A-gnostic. If that is true he just forgot to look up the meaning of the words Atheism and Materialism in a standard dictionary. But in a generally orthodox age they were terms of abuse, and he wanted to avoid them. To this day his followers make the same blunder and most mischievously encourage believers in their grotesque idea of the nature and consequences of Atheism and Materialism; and they praise "spiritual realities" in the usual ambiguous sense.

GLADSTONE

I have especially criticized these writers because they were all skeptics, not reactionaries, and gave great help in breaking the fetters of the old creeds, and because their ideas are not only shared by large numbers of skeptics but these men pose, ridiculously, as intellectually superior to Atheists and Materialists. Of the religious writers of high distinction in this period it is hardly necessary to speak, as their blunders are familiar. Let me give one illustration of how the old creeds still warped the mind. The British statesman, Gladstone, may be considered one of the ablest men of the last century who definitely belonged to the Christian fold and wrote admirably in defense of the faith. In a book, "The Impregnable Rock of Holy Scripture" (1890), which had an immense circulation, he shows how the old ideas still prevented men of high ability and great learning, only 50 years ago, from recognizing scientific truth. He, in unconscious imitation of the Pope (whom he detested) selects six modern ideas as false and damnable:

"1. That the discoveries of science as to natural objects have slain or destroyed the assertions of the early Scriptures with respect of the origin and history of the world and of man, its principal inhabitant.

"2. That their contents are in many cases offensive to the moral sense and humanity of an enlightened age.

"3. That our race made its appearance in the world in a condition but one degree above that of the brute creation, and only slow and painful but continuous progress has brought its representatives to the present phase of existence.

"4. That men have accomplished this by the exercise of their own natural powers and have never received the special teaching and authoritative guidance which is signified under the name of Divine Revelation.

"5. That the more considerable among the different races and nations of the world have devised and established from time to time their respective religions and in many cases accepted the promulgation of sacred books which are to be considered as essentially of the same character as the Bible.

"6. That the books of the Bible, and especially those of the Old Testament, which purport to be the earliest are far from being contemporary with the events which they record or with the authorities to whom they are ascribed."

Such was the final position of probably the ablest and most learned lay Christian in Europe half a century ago. Into what amusing blunders Gladstone was led in defending his position—in one famous bout he fought for the literal truth of the miracle of the Gadarene swine—with Huxley I need not tell here, but I may give a specimen of the general effect of this medieval faith on his culture. He was a master of Greek literature, and in a little known work, "Juventus Mundi, or The Gods and Men of the Heroic Age" (1869) he proves that the crude religion of the early Greeks that we find in Homer had hidden meanings and was a "precursor of the Christian religion." For instance he says of the trident of Poseidon (the Greek Neptune):

"With respect to the Trident, an instrument so unsuited to waters, it appears evidently to point to some tradition of the Trinity, such as may still be found in various forms of Eastern religion other than the Hebrew. It may have proceeded amongst the Phoenicians from the common source of an older tradition; and this seems more probable than a direct derivation from the Hebrews."

Educated London rocked with laughter. The trident of Greek and Roman mythologies is a fish-spear raised into a symbol of the god of the seas and is therefore particularly "suited to water."

Of attempts to found new religions—Theosophy, Christian Science, etc.—to meet the oncoming tide of Materialism I need not speak as we are considering the dumbness of the great not the artfulness of charlatans and fanatics. But a word must be said about Spiritualism. In a great debate, before 3,000 people, with Sir Arthur Conan Doyle in London, I started with the sentence: "Spiritualism was born of fraud cradled in fraud, and thrives on fraud today." Yet in the course of the last century it succeeded in duping men of great intellectual distinction. In the first 10 years of its fraudulent existence it claims to have captured several million followers in America, including a few judges and professors, and to have won the serious attention of men of still higher intellectual rank like Professor William James. It was then imported into Britain and later to the rest of Europe, and several men of at least great distinction in science embraced it with a credulity that seems incredible. Most important of these was Professor (later Sir) William Crookes, one of the leading chemists in Europe and the real discoverer—though he did not know it—of the electron. In the 70's of the last century a young woman adventurer of the crudest and most blatant type duped him for years. She masqueraded as the materialized form of the spirit of "Katie King," and in broad daylight she sat on his knee, was weighed in his machine, and so on, yet he continued to believe in her. When, in his last years, I challenged him to say whether he still believed in her he wrote me a pitifully evasive letter. Alfred Russel Wallace, the famous naturalist and codiscoverer of Natural Selection, was another and equally astonishing dupe. Another medium, whom any person of moderate intelligence ought to have been able to expose, seduced him into literal belief. In fact, his creed so warped his science that until he died he gave the greatest encouragement to the churches by flatly denying that man's mind, as well as his body, was evolved. The works of the last decade of his life are pitiful. The German Professor Zollner, though not in the class of these two, was another distinguished scientific dupe; deluded by the cheap adventurer Slade. Sir Oliver Lodge was another, but here we are departing far from the company of "the great." Late in the century, however, a new phase opened. The "phenomena" were pronounced to be genuine but were attributed to only "abnormal powers" of the medium. In this new superstition not only men like the distinguished astronomer Flammarion but men like Professor Richet, leading French physiologist, and Professor Lombroso, greatest European criminologist, were drawn. Even the able British critic and Ibsenite William Archer was drawn into the sheep-fold, as we may call it, before he died. We must certainly not omit these men from a record of the errors and absurdities of great minds. We get no encouragement or guidance from reading the eccentric ideas about the universe and the world of life that men formed in the ancient or the medieval world. In view of the scantiness of positive knowledge we understand. But the spectacle of eminent scientific men, masters of one branch of science betraying such credulity when they stray into other fields of knowledge is a warning for all time.

XIII.   OUR MODERN INFALLIBLE POPES

Heaven forbid that I should call any Pope in the entire series from the beginning of the 2nd century a "great" man. It is only by the excessive courtesy that historical writers now show to the Roman Church that even Gregory VII, Innocent III, Benedict XIV, and Leo XIII are paid the same homage as we more sincerely pay to the intellect of Frederick II, Voltaire, Napoleon, or Goethe. But since it has suited the Catholics of modern times to declare their Popes infallible, it is amusing to run over their monstrous blunders in the very field —the sphere of social, ethical, and doctrinal questions—in which they are understood to rise high above the wisdom of a congress of geniuses. Let me, with my usual neurotic scrupulousness, be perfectly just to our Catholic neighbors. It is only in certain conditions, in certain sharply defined utterances, that they claim infallibility for their great oracle. You may suggest that if I am sincere in my regard for justice I will confine myself to these utterances. But, alas, there are none. Nearly 80 years ago the Catholic hierarchy in more or less—we shall see the facts presently—solemn assembly at Rome declared that the Pope is infallible or cannot possibly make a mistake when he issues a declaration to his entire church on a point of faith or morals and makes it clear that he is drawing upon his prerogative of infallibility. But from that day (1870) to this no Pope has made any such declaration.

That is true, your Catholic friend will tell you, but it is also true that the declarations of the Popes always have a unique impressiveness. My professor of theology 60 years ago, who was a secret Modernist, told me that the Catholic bishops who in 1870 opposed this dogma of infallibility—he had known a number of them—used to say, with a flippancy that shocks us, that it meant that "the Pope has the Holy Ghost in his inkpot." Now is it likely that the Holy Ghost should wait—I nearly said hibernate—in the golden inkpot into which the Pope never dips and be completely indifferent to what blunders he makes when dipping into his other ink pots to give the world the guidance for which it pants? Curiously enough that never occurs to your Catholic neighbor. However not only he but your daily or weekly paper, which in intervals between its comic strips and its advertisements of ladies' undies talks about the Venerable Head of the greatest Church, the Holy See, the Sovereign Pontiff, and so on, tells you that there is a unique force or wisdom in all that the Pope says. The Vatican has the most cosmopolitan and most costly intelligence service in the world. Its antennae reach from Hudson's Bay to Patagonia, from Boston to Auckland. And the Pope, surrounded by a cabinet of cardinals from all countries, is the one man out of 200,000,000 who has been chosen for his wisdom and virtue . . . If you have read my "History of the Popes," you'll smile. But here, as I have passed the 18th century, I must confine myself to the last 10 Popes.

Ever since the French Revolution the mind of the race has boiled and seethed with questions, but after the fall of Napoleon and the restoration of feudalism, which from the angle of a humane economics means savagery, Rome thought for 30 years that the world had returned to the Middle Ages and it left the Holy Ghost out of account in choosing its Popes. It didn't matter much, as the work was done by a series of Secretaries of State, cardinals who were as memorable for their blondes and their palaces as they were for their success in money-making. There was Pope Leo (1823-9), nearly a senile wreck—though he was still able to shoot birds in the Vatican Garden—at whom the whole of Europe mocked. Then there was Pius VIII (1829-30), who *was* a senile wreck, shuffling, paralyzed, about the palace for a few months. Next came Gregory XVI (1830-45), a vulgar gluttonous man who for 15 years enjoyed candy, strong wine, spicy gossip, and the erotic novels of Paul de Kook, while he had 6,000 rebels against the foul condition of his kingdom tortured in his jails. And then came the man whom Catholics now call "the Venerable" Pope Pius IX; the man who bullied the bishops into declaring him infallible, but who made more blunders, in an age that seethed with problems, than any other Pope since the Reformation during his 30 years of rule.

He was elected in 1846, when Europe was boiling up for the Revolutions of 1848, and in his small-minded bewilderment he at first coquetted flutteringly with the Liberals. Revolution soon swept him from his throne and he fled from Rome. From his comfortable exile he brooded bucolically over this heaving new world, where brutal armies were now driving the people back into slavery and thousands were murdered because they wanted freedom and democracy, and the only remedy this supreme guide of the age could think of was to declare solemnly the dogma of the Immaculate Conception; which led to the extraordinary imposture, later officially blessed by the Pope, of the apparition of the Virgin at Lourdes. It is not a specimen of blunders of the great but of the great blunders of the little. And so he blundered for 30 years, while Europe, which he cursed periodically, "rounded onward to the light," and the number of victims in the foul Papal jails rose to 8,000. He violently denounced the toleration of Protestantism and Bible Societies in Italy. His own Papal States were then, the British ambassador said, "the opprobrium of Europe," while Rome was described by the famous French priest Lamennais as "the foulest sewer that had ever been opened to the eye of man." He brooded over the "anarchy" of the world, which we now recognize as the birth-pangs of at least a better civilization, and with owl-like wisdom he concluded that "Liberalism" was the fetid swamp from which all the poisons and devils emanated. So he got his Jesuits to formulate in 80 propositions these poisonous sentiments of wicked literature and advanced politics, and he drew them up solemnly in a "Syllabus" and declared them "reprobated, proscribed, and condemned." American readers of Msgr Ryan and Fulton Sheen might be surprised that here are some of the propositions solemnly condemned by the head of their church as late as 1864:

"Philosophy must be treated without taking any account of supernatural religion.

"Every man is free to embrace and profess the religion which, judging by the light of human reason, he believes to be true.

"Men may find the way of salvation and attain it in any religion.

"We may entertain at least a well-founded hope of the eternal salvation of all those who do not belong to the true Church of Christ.

"The best theory of civil society requires that popular schools . . . and educational institutions generally . . . should be freed from all ecclesiastical authority . . .

"The Church ought to be separated from the State and the State from the Church.

"It is allowable to refuse to obey and even rebel against legitimate princes (as America had done).

"By the law of nature the marriage-tie is not indissoluble.

"The Roman Pontiff can and ought to reconcile himself to and agree with progress, liberalism, and modern civilization."

His defiance of the modern age roused such ferocious enthusiasm throughout the church, such spasms of breathless admiration of his wisdom, that he began to prepare the way for the declaration of his infallibility.

The Vatican Council, which met in 1869 mainly to promulgate this dogma, was preceded by five years of intrigue and inquiry throughout the church as to whether it was safe and advisable to launch such a monstrous doctrine, and it was the most human and most heated general council of the church for many centuries. As early as 1867 more than 500 bishops were consulted. The Holy Ghost did not take a back seat; he was nowhere near the preparations for this proposition which was eventually presented to the world in his name. There was a heavy opposition and some free speech. My professor told me that gallons of iced water had to be passed round every day. But between bribery and intimidation the opposition—save for a rump which seceded and founded the Old Catholic Church—was worn down, and the dogma was declared. But Pius put away his infallible robes in camphor and continued his blundering to the end of his days. I need give only two specimens. In 1869 he heard that a girls' college in which science was taught had ben opened in France. He wrote to the bishop of Montpellier (December, 22) about "the vice of an institution which prepares for social life not only good mothers of families at the height of their mission but women swollen with pride by a vain and impotent science." He went on:

"Science cannot guard them against the public dangers to which the more delicate sex is exposed . . . It is deplorable that to the various means hitherto employed to corrupt the faith of your people there is now added an institution for destroying the faith of the adolescent."

Even the Catholic papers of France resented this; as they did again when in 1874 he condemned the use of the Roman classical literature in Latin classes. In 1877 the old man learned that some wicked guy named Darwin had (18 years earlier) advanced a theory of evolution. His letter—again to a French bishop—is so carefully buried that a few years ago the famous Oxford scholar, Dr. Coulton, got the head of the British Museum to ask me to find it, and I had great difficulty. It runs on these lines:

"The theory would seem to need no refutation did not alienation from God and the leaning toward Materialism, due to depravity, eagerly seek a support in all this tissue of fables . . . In fact, pride, after rejecting the Creator of all things and proclaiming man independent, wishing him to be his own king, his own priest, and his own God—this pride goes so far as to degrade man to the level of the unreasoning brutes, perhaps even of lifeless matter ... But the corruption of the age, the machinations of the perverse, the danger of the simple, demand that such fancies, altogether absurd as they are—since they bear the mark of sin—be refuted by true science."

After this the infallible blunderer went to his reward, and the cardinals met to elect a man who really would give guidance to an increasingly troubled world. A year or so later I was, as a boy in a Catholic school, compelled to bow in reverence before "the skull cap of Pius IX." It was probably one of thousands ordered by the Vatican, airily blessed in a heap by the Pope, and sold at $5,000 or so each over the Catholic world. But they couldn't, or didn't think it safe to, get up any miracles, so Pius is only a Half-Saint.

Then, in 1878, came Leo XIII, whom the press and literature of the world have accepted as a great Pope, a most profound counsellor of a troubled age. He was a clever and, from the literary angle, a quite accomplished man. An elderly Belgian aristocrat once told me a story of the days when as a cardinal he was stationed in Belgium. At a reception in Brussels a wicked Liberal count, introduced to him, presented his snuff-box, open, to the cardinal. On the inside of the lid a nude lady was painted. The cardinal blandly took a pinch and asked, smiling: "The countess, I suppose?" He was detested by Pius IX, of whose intelligence he must have had a fair estimate, yet he was, relatively to his age, almost as great a blunderer as Pius.

The Papacy faced two big problems. The Italians had taken Rome and the Papal States—as a matter of fact, the people had voted in a crushing majority for inclusion in the kingdom of Italy—and the French had just recovered from the mood of synthetic piety into which the Communard scare of 1871 had driven them—just as the Communist scare drives them into political alliance with the Vatican today—and were quitting the Church in vast numbers. On both points the Pope blundered tragically and nearly lost Italy and France. He excommunicated the "robbers," the Italian King and statesmen, and declared himself a "prisoner" in the Vatican. I will admit that this melodramatic fiction started the great flow of gold from America to Rome, but anticlericalism captured half of Italy. Leo refused to recognize the republican government of France until it secularized the country and completely broke the power of the church. He repeatedly affronted America (which, apart from Catholics, smiled) by denouncing divorce as "legalized concubinage" and the separation of state and church as an inspiration of the devil; and when he found that the American bishops and archbishops were explaining in America that their branch of the church was more liberal than the Italian he published a most offensive "open letter" to those prelates (1899), almost accusing them of heresy and commanding them to toe the line—which they did. They make the same plea far more boldly and untruthfully today, of course, but the American Catholic Church—it is dropping the title Roman—of our time is 1,000 times as rich as it was in 1900. Curious how that modulates the accents of the oracle.

He blundered on every side. Ireland was desperately poor and sent little to Rome, but England was rich and Leo dreamed of bringing it over to Catholicism. The British diplomats fooled him. Hinting at gratitude they complained that the Irish were virtually in a state of rebellion against their British rulers, and the Pope ordered the Irish to abandon their Protestant leader Parnell and their Fenian Society (1883). The Poles were as rebellious against Russia as the Irish were against England, and in the hope of getting concessions from Russia he ordered the Poles to submit (1886); and he got no more from Russia than from England.

Catholic scholars were being shamed into drawing some sort of modern veil over the rawness of their faith. Repeatedly and solemnly, in fact truculently, he ordered that all Catholic seminaries and universities must confine themselves to philosophy as it had been taught by Thomas Aquinas in the depths of the Middle Ages, and any professors who did not at once submit lost their jobs. He found scholars chafing at the tissue of lies and legends which passed as ecclesiastical history, and (1883) he issued an encyclical letter in which he boasted that no modern historians were equal to Baronius and Muratori, and that the church insisted that its historical writers should tell all truth! In a magnificent gesture he threw open the "secret archives" of the Vatican to scholars of the world; but the leading Catholic historian, L. Pastor, tells us that he found that the really secret documents were first removed. He enforced the Index of Prohibited Books (1897); and, as Putman shows, it still contained monstrous errors and condemned half the best literature of Europe. He in 1902 established a Biblical Commission, to tell the world the very truth about the Bible. My old professor of theology (a secret Modernist and scandalous trimmer) was secretary of it; and it endorsed the most pitifully medieval ideas about the Bible. I heard on sound authority after Leo's death that in his last delirious hours he kept repeating: "That biblical question, that biblical question!" As a final trial of such historical scholars as were left in the church, he, in 1894, endorsed the popular Italian belief in the "Holy House of Loreto"; a legend that after the death of Mary this cottage of hers had been brought by angels from Judea to Italy and set up at Loreto!

Ignoring or hiding all these facts, though nearly all of them are found in the semi-official life of Leo by Msgr. T. Serclaes, Catholic sophists in America like Msgr. Ryan put Leo before their readers as the most luminous moral oracle of the last century on the ground of his "great" encyclicals. I have shown elsewhere that Ryan tampers with the translation, but even as he gives them, the boast of wisdom is ridiculous and the real purpose is misrepresented. They chiefly relate to political and labor questions. Before the end of his first year Leo attacked politics. He fell fiercely on "those men who call themselves by the barbaric names of Socialists, Communists, and Nihilists," as if there were any common ground of Socialism and Nihilism. There was then little Socialism outside Germany, and the gauntlet was flung—it was really a deal with Bismarck to shift persecution from the Catholics—at the Social Democrats of Prussia. What was the result? The Catholic vote, relatively to population, fell year by year, and the Socialist vote rose rapidly. Fifteen years later the Pope felt that he must approach the matter differently. He issued the Encyclical *Rerum Novarum* on labor, which Catholics have put on record as The Charter of Labor. It is one long catalogue of the Liberal opinions which Pius had branded, though they had now become platitudes. The press, other than Labor, filled columns with comment on the extraordinary fact that the Pope had declared that the worker was entitled to a "decent" or "living" wage. What a comment on his own church that it had taken 18 centuries to discover that! But when, as Msgr. T. Serclaes tells us, the Pope, though pressed, refused to say what the living wage is—even the employer of sweated labor says that he gives it—and when Leo sourly withdrew in his later years all concessions to the workers, the world-press was silent. So is Ryan.

As to the other "great" Encyclical *Immortale Dei,* or "On the Christian Constitution of States," it is simply a rebuke to the French for disestablishing the church and secularizing the schools, and it is therefore in effect an insult to America. Before the end of 1878 he had started on this line:

"By a new sort of impiety that was unknown even to the pagans they set up governments without any regard for God or the order established by him. They proclaim that public authority does not derive from God . . . but from the people."

He returned to it in an Encyclical of 1881 "On the Origin of Civil Power." Then when France became a purely secular state, he let off the fireworks of *Immortale Dei*. Ryan, in praising its mixture of platitudes and Scholasticism, carefully conceals one fact; that Leo insists that not merely religion, but the Roman religion, must be the foundation of states: Naturally they must be based upon *true* religion, and then:

"As to the question which religion is the true one, it is not difficult for any man of prudence and sincerity. There are innumerable and brilliant proofs—the truth of the prophecies, the crowd of martyrs, the prodigious speed of the spread of the faith amongst its enemies and in spite of great obstacles, the witness of the martyrs, and other arguments."

He props up with these worm-eaten myths of the Middle Ages a thesis which America rejects, and Catholic literature, skillfully, touching up the Encyclical, presents it to America as the most profound and sublime political document of the last century . . . What a pity Leo (or any other Pope) did not know that, as American Catholic writers now say, we moderns derive our idea of democracy from the Jesuit writers Suarez and Bellarmine of 300 years ago. The real reason that Popes never said so, is not, of course, because it is false, but because until 70 years ago they regarded democracy as inspired rather by the devil than by the Jesuits.

Let it not be said that I represent Leo XIII to have been a fool, any more than I represented Aristotle as a fool in describing his blunders. A man's opinions must be judged by the world-fund of knowledge in his time. These Popes shut their eyes to the new wisdom and blasphemed it. I notice them here only because not only Catholic literature but almost the entire press of America assures the public that the Vatican is a rich storehouse of wisdom and the whole world should appreciate the golden words of Popes.

The Vatican lost immensely more subjects under Leo XIII than in the time of the Reformation in spite of the fact that Leo compromised on moral principles wherever an advantage to the church was offered; and he was nearly always duped by the statesmen. At the time of his death (1903) the world was passing into the new and dangerous phase which culminated in two terrible world-wars and the monstrous load of tragedies and problems that crushes our age. And the cardinals, who got together and implored the light of the Holy Ghost, elected a man of the old Chinese mandarin type. He lived in the center of the world as if he were blind and deaf. He worked only for the church, founding Catholic Action (1905), issuing (1907) the decree *Ne Temere* which affronted civil powers everywhere by insisting that Catholics observe in regard to marriage provisions of the Canon Law that are against all civil law, and in the same year launching a campaign against Modernism in the church which drove out or drove into hypocrisy its best scholars. This narrow-minded Pope, Pius X, issued a gold medal (the Pope slaying the dragon of Modernism) to celebrate his victory over truth: just as a predecessor had issued a gold medal to commemorate the St. Bartholomew Massacre.

Benedict XV (1914-22) was an abler man but just as futile from the angle of world-guidance. The first World War, to the approach of which his predecessors had been completely blind, at once raged round him, and he was as helpless as any French peasant who saw bombs dropping around him. Indeed it was not long before the Italians, who were then fighting the Austrians, found and published proof that the Vatican was in communication with the enemy and was tampering with the loyalty of Catholic soldiers. Like Leo XIII he was duped by the promises of German diplomats; and like the present Pope he began to appeal for peace when it became clear that Germany could not win.

Pius XI (1922-39), who succeeded him, passed into history as the moral oracle who made the infamous compact with Mussolini for $90,000,000 and other great advantages to the church, blessed the vile design of General Franco to plunge Spain into civil war, and let the Germans and Italians perform the curtain-raiser of the second World

War. He was the man who radioed over the world the poisonous call to a crusade against Atheistic Communism, on the ground of which Hitler and Mussolini, pretending that this was their sole objective, persuaded France and Britain to stand aside while Germany made its formidable preparations and German and Italian troops practiced butchery in Spain. He it was who, bringing up to date, he said, the grand encyclical of Leo XIII on labor, in a new encyclical (*Quadragesimo anno*) retracted such concessions as Leo seemed to make and bade Catholic workers everywhere accept the idea of a Corporative State on the Fascist model; while Msgr. Ryan was dangling before the eyes of America this gem from one of the Pope's messages:

"The Church does not desire, neither ought she to desire, to mix up without a just cause in the direction of purely civic affairs."

Ryan has proudly translated for Americans the 10 encyclicals of this wonderful moral guide of the world in one of its most dangerous and most fateful periods (1923-29). After his initial general discourse on the wickedness and blindness of the world they are as follows:

On the Centenary of St. Francis de Sales.
On the Centenary of Thomas Aquinas.
On the Centenary of St. Jehosaphat.
On the Cultural Associations set up in France.
On the Feast of Our Lord Jesus Christ the King.
On Catholic missions.
On Francis of Assisi.
On the Persecution of the Church in Mexico.

Curtain.

But long before this wooly-minded "statesman" had passed to the Bosom of Abraham, the present Pope, Pius XII, then Cardinal Pacelli, had become Secretary of State and really ruled the church. He was the chief architect of the policy that linked the Vatican with the Fascist, Nazi, and Japanese thugs, and history will probably say that he ought to have been in the dock at Nuremberg with their chief leaders. He was raised to his position in 1930. This was the year after the Vatican's Concordat with Mussolini, but this had been followed by serious friction. What Pacelli did to end this may be judged from the fact that in 1932 the King of Italy decorated him with the highest order of nobility at his disposal, and the Vatican awarded its highest honors to the King.

In the same year the Vatican ordered the German bishops to forbid their people to oppose Hitler and so gave him his first majority. Next year Hitler rewarded (as far as he ever did reward anybody who helped him) the Vatican with a Concordat, while he slaughtered the Jews, Socialists, and Communists, and strangled democracy. In 1934, Pacelli, having established in Europe an order that was bound to eventuate in war, went to South America and induced those long-standing and bitter enemies of the church, the Liberals, to join with it and the other reactionaries and set up a Fascist regime in nearly all the republics. He passed on to the United States, won the heart of Cardinal Mundelein and others (who threw all their weight on his side in the later Papal election), and built a new pipe-line for gold from America to Rome. In 1935 he saw Mussolini brutally invade Abyssinia and the whole Italian Church flame with joy; and he said nothing. In 1936 he received General Franco at the Vatican, but, of course, we don't know the burden of their private conversations. All that we know is that when Franco rebelled in July the Vatican was the first foreign power to hoist his pirate flag and the Papal banner was the first foreign flag to wave over Franco's headquarters at Burgos; and from that summer to the tragic end he rejoiced in the martyrdom of the Spanish people and gave the Catholic world one grossly untruthful message after another about the nature of the struggle. And after all this blessed work for the pacification of the earth, what could the cardinals—British and American, French, Italian, German, etc.—do but declare him chosen by the Holy Ghost for the spiritual rule of the world?

Professor Salvemini (of Harvard) has proved to the satisfaction of every scholar his complicity with Mussolini. I have shown by such a heap of quotations from, mostly, Catholic sources his appalling guilt in supporting the German and the Japanese plan that Catholics induced Washington, on the plea that little I was disturbing the grand unity of the nation in the war-effort, to suppress the chief work in which I did this; and the pious authorities of New York port attempted to close their gates against the importation from Britain of other works in which I do the same. I hope they got their gold medal blessed by the Pope. The rest of the Pope's sacred oracles—on biblical studies, on the Mystic Body of Christ, on St. Cyril of Alexandria, etc.—do not interest me; nor is this the place to describe how, after the two years silence to allow the people to forget how he had backed Mussolini, Franco, Hitler, and Matsuoka, he has emerged in the different-colored robe of an ally of America and Britain in the crusade to impose democracy (which he loathes) upon the world. "Peace" is still the most tender refrain on his lips; and he is fostering the grave risk of civil war in France and Italy and supporting with all his power of intrigue the worst elements in America, Britain, and France who are working for the speedy inauguration of the third World War.

Indeed, by this time some of my readers will be wondering what the Popes are doing in this galley at all. Do I call these things dumbness? Or do I call the Popes great? But if they look back they will see that the sub-title of this book announces a record of all sorts of aberrations of "the world's outstanding leaders." If I include the moral mistakes of moralists like Emerson and Carlyle—honest mistakes in the belief that they are for the good of the race—how much more must I include these perversities of the world's greatest professional moralists? As to their "greatness," not only nine folk out of 10 but nine-tenths of the world press and literature will assure you that our Emersons and Carlyles were, as moral and social guides, pygmies in comparison with these almost-inspired oracles. You may care at least to learn in detail the stark contrast between what even the New York *Times* and the *Herald-Tribune*, to say nothing about the Chicago *Tribune*, and the heads of our leading universities tell you about the matter and the reality.

XIV. OTHER MODERN ORACLES

One would think that when we reach the full light and the complete freedom of criticism of the 20th century we should find few men of distinction perpetrating the blunders, eccentricities of opinion, or absurdities of which I have given an historic survey. On the contrary, if I were to continue here my practice of quoting such aberrations in the words of the writers themselves I should not have space left to deal with more than a tithe of the authors I propose to impeach. The world's literature, in fact, was never before so rich in recriminations and charges of blithering idiocy as it is today. And this reminds us at once of the relativity of such charges. Hitherto I have described statements as absurd, judged by the received knowledge of our age. But our age is so terrifically divided in its creeds—religious, social, political, and economic—that of even two distinguished writers the sublime truth of one is medieval rubbish to the other. To the American devotee of Free Enterprise the work of the ablest Russian economist is moonshine: to the Marxian the professors of economics at the most important American universities utter tripe. To the spiritist Materialism is a superficial, utterly false, and profoundly mischievous froth of words, while the Materialist thinks, like Zeno of old and most of the Greek thinkers, that "to talk of spirit is to talk of nothing." Where shall we, to use Einsteinian language, find the ideal or "absolute" observation point?

Clearly in political and economic and many other controversies it is impossible to do so. At all events I will make no attempt to do so here. All that we can do is to recognize that we have in our time a vast body of proved and accepted scientific and historical truth and judge writers by this. And since scientists, when engaged on their proper work without the adulteration of their thoughts with other interests, and historians, while they may in face of such new phenomena such as the discovery of radiation throw out theories or guesses that are later discarded, do not offer us nonsense or absurdities, like Aristotle's "matter and form" or Descartes' pineal soul, I quote few of these. To be sure, even distinguished scientists are apt to talk nonsense when they quit the field of which each is a master. In one of the works of that brilliant astronomer, Sir James Jeans, for instance, I found a casual reference to "the lung of a fly," and everybody is familiar with their pathetic blunders when they declare their opinions on history, politics, economics, or social questions. They trample like a herd of elephants on a poor "popularizer" like myself who has spent 60 years gleaning in their various fields truths that bear upon one's philosophy of life instead of mastering every cell in the body of a frog or every type of rock in the earth's crust, yet they seem often to think that they may dogmatize on a range of subjects, from the ethic of Jesus to the Bolshevik Revolution, without having made any such comprehensive study.

However, it is when they allow some other interest, generally religion, to warp their minds that they fall into real absurdities. In one of his ablest works ("The Scientific Basis of Evolution," p. 254) one of the most distinguished of American scientists, Professor T. H. Morgan, falls heavily upon the sophists, not of old times or even the last century, but his own time in America. In a scornful reference to the anti-Mechanists (or anti-Materialists) he says:

"The boldest spirits among the Mechanists further claim that in time they hope to bring within reach of their methods a study of the lucubrations, hallucinations, and obsessions of the human mind which, masquerading under the illumination of introspective metaphysics and transcendental philosophy, pretend to solve all the riddles of the universe."

That fine zoologist and humanist, Sir. P. Chalmers Mitchell, even says ("Materialism and Vitalism in Biology," p. 3) that this plague has been worse than ever in the last 30 years. There is a "pragmatic effort to load the dice of scientific data with emotional professions," he says, and "the primitive myth-making faculty has re-awakened." The eminent scientists, you notice, scarify their opponents in a way that a gentle critic like myself never does. I will give later some examples of the modern ideas of the outstanding sophists—"eagles do not catch flies," remember —which they have in mind.

If this is the character of the able men whom our leading scientists condescend to notice, what are we likely to find in the rag-tag-and-bobtail of the enormous religious literature of our time? Naturally the more medieval the doctrines they seek to reconcile with or prove superior to modern science the worse the absurdities which they perpetrate. In other words, it is particularly Catholic literature that is rich in such matters. I will not here quote any of the popular editors or men who, like Fulton Sheen, talk the more glibly because they are not hampered by any sort of scholarship. My books are full of their meanderings. I would advise the reader to save time by sampling the cream. In 1910 the American Catholic Church spent hundreds of thousands of dollars on a Catholic Encyclopedia in which it promised us the finest scholarship that it could command in America and Europe. You will find its historical articles (lives of Popes, saints, marytrs, etc.), if you know history, as fictional as Grimm's fairy tales or the travels of

Baron Munchausen. You will find the few articles on science just the old Thomas Aquinas stuff, and the exposition of Catholic doctrine in some places eviscerated but as a rule just the old robust stuff thinly sophisticated. I quote just two specimens. In the article "Evolution," a scientific doctrine then accepted by all the experts in the world, we have such gems as:

"There is no evidence whatever for the common descent of all plants and animals from a single primitive organism . . . Haeckel's phylogeny is at almost no point supported by experiment and observation . . . Our leading scientists do not care to support the unfounded generalities of Haeckel's doctrines . . . The central idea of modern evolutionary theories—namely, progressive specialization and development—has not up to the present received any confirmation from observation of the world of organisms as it now exists . . . Paleontology can assert nothing whatever of the development of the body of men from the animal."

The other quotation is a few sentences from the article "Tolerance," a noble offering to folk who live under the American Constitution:

"A person who is tolerant in the domain of dogma resembles the botanist who cultivates in his experimental beds both edible plants and poisonous herbs as alike valuable growths, while a person intolerant of error may be compared to a market gardener who allows only edible plants to grow and eradicates noxious weeds [Protestants and Skeptics] . . . The 'freedom of thought' claimed by Freethinkers is really vitiated by an internal contradiction, since the intellect is bound by the laws of thought and must in any case yield to the force of evidence . . . Nowhere is dogmatic intolerance so necessary as a rule of life as in the domain of religious belief, since for an individual his eternal salvation is at stake . . . It is just in this exclusiveness that lies the Church's unique strength, the stirring power of her propaganda, the unfailing vigor of her progress. A strictly logical consequence of this incontestable fundamental idea is the ecclesiastical dogma that outside the Church there is no salvation."

If you want to understand the childishness of the beliefs that several not unknown Americans have embraced in the last few years spend an hour or two examining this reservoir of sour pap. Special marks are due for the audacity of the phrase "the vigor of her progress." A few years earlier I had proved in my "Decay of the Church of Rome" that it had lost 80,000,000 members in the preceding 80 years.

The Fundamentalists are, of course, as bad as the Catholics in regard to science, but if I began to quote these I should be reminded that this is supposed to be a book about the dumbness of the *great*. Modernist literature has a different kind of absurdity. It proceeds on the same high principle as modern art. You may not be sure at first glance whether a picture represents a race-horse, a hay-stack, or a liver-sausage, but use your mind on it and read a meaning into it. So Jesus was sublime even when he taught the doctrine of hell; he merely meant the Turkish Bath at the gates of Paradise where dirty folk are scrubbed clean before mingling with the angels. The gospel is not false when it says the women found a bright young-man angel in the tomb of Jesus; they mistook a ray of the rising sun penetrating the dark tomb for an angel. And so on. The evolution of religion is quite true. In these advancing savage cults and then the series of religions and sacred books in the civilized period we just have a "Progressive Revelation." God revealed his glory in stages (spread over 100,000 years) which were nicely adapted to the degree of intelligence of the race at each stage. The first stage is that of the Australian aboriginal who says that the explanation of rain is that Mumbo Jumbo above . . .

As to the fancy religions that appeared, like fungi round a rotting tree—Spiritualism, Christian Science, Theosophy, Theophilanthropy,

Positivism, etc.—the searcher for absurdities would here have a delectable time, but I must be brief. In one comprehensive absurdity they all agree. No writer of any one of them dare admit the evolution of the "mind," which is certain in science. Every religion vitally assumes that what is popularly called "the mind" is a distinct reality from, though mysteriously connected with, the brain, and of a fundamentally different character than matter. That belief is dead in psychology, the specific science of "the mind," and is completely refuted by the evidence of man's evolution.

And this final and irreconcilable—it defies even the verbiage of the Modernist—clash of science and religion led to the few developments of what we must frankly call absurdities in the works of several distinguished men of science of our time. One is the attempt to prolong the life of that piece of medieval verbiage called Vitalism: the theory that the "vital principle" of all living things is immaterial. It was now called Neo-Vitalism, but there was nothing new about it, except that it fell back upon the phraseology of Aristotle rather than that of the medieval theologians. Dr. H. F. Osborn, curator of the Natural History Museum, was one of the most outspoken Vitalists in America. As a paleontologist (an authority on fossils) his opinion on this biological question was of no value, and when he was challenged to quote proper authorities he made matters worse ("The Earth Speaks to Byron"). He mentioned Millikan and Lodge (two physicists), Eucken (a theologian), Driesch (a philosopher), W. Rathenuau (a German businessman), and "Professor J. B. S. Haldane" (in which he confuses Professor J. B. S. Haldane the Materialist, with his father, Dr. J. B. Haldane, who moreover, Haldane told me, resented being called a Vitalist). Bergson's fantastic work "Creative Evolution," which was as much talked about 30 years ago as a popular novel, was based entirely on Vitalism, which is now dead in science.

For an analysis of this piece of verbiage which justifies one in calling it an absurdity I must refer to other works of mine. It was just the first line of defense against the Materialism that was steadily advancing in the last century. When it began to crumble rapidly, 36 to 40 years ago, under the disdain of physiologists, another scientist with mystic beliefs to defend, Lloyd Morgan, rector of a Welch university, thought out an even greater absurdity. "Emergent Evolution." When the Materialists advanced over the decaying Vitalism and captured the world of life the mystics began to wonder if they would not dare to go in to attack that citadel of spiritual realities, the mind of man. Discoveries of new prehistoric remains every decade made this inevitable. Very well, said the mystics. Let the evolutionists claim the whole realm of life, but the mind had a singular sort of evolution. It "emerged" from the vasty deeps and is not the mind of the ape in a higher stage. This blatant contradiction in terms was snapped up by Dr. H. F. Osborn. He made it still more ridiculous by daring to say just when the soul of man "emerged" and joined the ape-man body. The "wonderful" art of cave-man—it is at the Eskimo level in reality—shows that at that stage wholly new powers had come to man. New York friends of mine who knew Osborn well told me that the drawing-room atmosphere, which he loved, had more to do than mysticism with his views. We may, however, remember that the Fundamentalists were then pressing him hard with the charge that science is materialistic.

MENDEL

The appearance of Mendelism also at the beginning of the century led many scientific men into deplorable blunders. It at first claimed that the Darwinian idea of natural selection gradually accentuating small natal variations was discredited because it was discovered that large changes occurred at birth and these were the cause of new species. They were called "mutations" and the theory Mutationism. As it is now admitted that these are rare and generally ineffective, the name is dropped. But in the study of the cause of them a real science of heredity took shape, and, as it was now found that an odd sort of skeptic, Mendel, who had become the abbot of a monastery, had discovered some of the facts—and scientists today have a laudable desire to please the church—the science took his name, Mendelism. It is now the valuable science of Genetics, and its devotees look back with embarrassment on the language their predecessors used. Nature (heredity) was everything and nurture (environment) nothing. Darwinism was "as dead as the dodo." The churches were illuminated and their bells rang out merrily. Amateur sociologists (Bernard Shaw, etc.) took it up and said that attempts to train children were "a vile abortion." It is, Professor Karl Pearson said, settled in the fertilized ovum whether the child will be "good" or "bad." And so on. A monstrous amount of nonsense was poured out between 1910 and 1930. Those of us who, like myself, refused to be in fashion were heavily rebuked by the professors. Today it is generally acknowledged that environment and heredity are equally important factors. In the case of man, in fact, the new science of social psychology throws by far the greater stress on environment.

JEANS AND EDDINGTON

The blunders of certain distinguished physicists and astronomers were far more mischievous. The late Sir James Jeans and Sir Arthur Eddington were two of the most brilliant mathematical astronomers and physicists in Europe. I have not found that any distinguished physicist took up their ideas in America, and indeed their British colleagues often treated them severely (in review of their works in *Nature*). It was mainly the churches that sent their publications into one edition after another, though the cold silence or acrid censures of many of their colleagues ought to have warned them that they had discovered a mare's nest. But Eddington was a devout Quaker, Jeans a member of the Church of England, and their belief that they had found a way to discredit Materialism finally and completely put blinkers on their minds. As most of my readers will know, their contention was that Materialists hold that the atoms of matter are not composed of smaller parts and would never break up into something else. I have shown repeatedly that, not only had the supposed arch-Materialist Haeckel expressly claimed in his "Riddle of the Universe" 50 years ago that an atom is a close cluster of much smaller particles of something, but that the best American manuals of physics declare this to have been the general opinion of physicists since Crookes's experiments 20 years earlier, and that Lester F. Ward gave it as "one of the two chief physical theories" in America. Ward even said that some held (in 1880) that the atom was compacted of energy.

The only other point on which these two brilliant sophists of our time agreed may not unjustly be described as an utter absurdity. In their general philosophy they fell back upon the most absurd theory of Bishop Berkeley that *there are no material realities*; that what we call such are only ideas in the mind of God. Whatever philosophers say of this theory you have only to reflect that it means that there are no wars, no economic orders, no problems, etc., and that what these two erratic geniuses would consider the ugliest of things—sexual organs, license, cruelty, toilets, etc.—are ideas in the divine mind. This seems to make it incredible that they really meant what I have ascribed to them but in scientific interviews published in the chief British Sunday paper *The Observer* (December 21, 1930 and January 4, 1931) they expressly admitted it. Jeans piled absurdity upon absurdity when in several books he assured the religious world that it followed from the new physics that the material universe—the universe in which he did not believe—had had a beginning and had therefore been created.

After this it is not necessary to quote our philosophers. In fact, no one will venture to accuse of "absurdity" such men as Dewey and Whitehead, but one can have a good deal of sympathy with the distinguished scientist (already quoted) who calls their ideas "lucubrations, hallucinations, and obsessions of the human mind." In one respect only I would venture to use the word absurdity about the works of contemporary philosophers, and this applies also to many professors of ethics, to say nothing of the great majority of the writers who invoke or discuss moral ideals. All of them rely on "intuition," and it is a medieval myth. Modern psychology, which after decades of observation and experiment, describes for us the whole "contents of the mind," as we used to say, has rejected it. Yet you will find distinguished literary men and scientists as well as philosophers and theologians appealing to or relying on it as if it were as real as memory. In the light of our present knowledge of man's brain-life it is a patent absurdity, yet no other fallacy of the old days survives so abundantly in modern literature as this does.

I can do no more in this chapter than summarize contemporary errors and absurdities with which I have dealt fully in earlier works, and I confine myself still to condemnation only in cases where we have a large body of settled expert opinion to which the critic can appeal. If I were to say here what I think of much that our psychoanalysts and psychiatrists say, I might be accused of prejudice and would at least not have a generally received body of knowledge to appeal to. In regard to political, social, economic, and ethical questions in detail anything I could say about the opinions of others would have only a personal value. There is, perhaps, one point that arises from the preceding paragraph, on which one may venture to speak of absurdity. We talk of moral law every day, yet half the folk who write most eloquently about it are vague or confused as to its nature. There are, in academic works, three theories of it. It is either a Christian code of conduct, a social code, or something that "our conscience teaches us" or the mind perceives in some mystic way. Since there is no such thing as intuition, the third idea is absurd, yet it is still amazingly common amongst not only literary men and moralists but even scientific men and historians. It seems to haunt the mind only because it has been deeply imprinted on it by education and is maintained by our literature. The point may seem academic but it is far otherwise. Apart from convinced Christians, this is the main ground of quarrels about sexual behavior and moral censorships.

PROFESSOR ARNOLD TOYNBEE

In the province of history few outstanding authorities could be charged with anything like absurdity. It might seem strained even to suggest the possibility of distinguished experts making absurd statements in their own fields but I have already given several instances of authorities of the first rank in science being diverted into that unfortunate position by their religious opinions. There is at least one such instance in the historical field in our time, and the name of the historian, Professor Arnold Toynbee, seems to be in the highest regard in American universities. During his 1947 tour of those universities Professor Toynbee did not obtrude this theory of his which I have in mind, but it is sufficiently indicated in his chief work, and it is developed at length and emphatically asserted in a special lecture (the Burge Lecture) which he gave in England to a body of Christian students. It is the monstrous idea that since religion has gained by all collapses of civilization we should look forward at least with equanimity to the collapse of civilization in our time which so many folk predict. If I may not call that an absurdity I will call it a monstrosity of mysticism. In fact the historical statement itself, that collapses of civilization led to a rise or increase of influence of religion, is ridiculously false in the sense in which Professor Toynbee affirms it. He is, of course, thinking of the complete capture of Europe by Christianity after the fall of Rome. It is obvious that he has a totally false idea of the quality of the religion and the character of the people of the Dark Age. Was this appalling degradation, which lasted centuries, a compensation for the destruction of the Roman civilization? Similarly with other collapses (China, India, Spain, etc.) They were always followed by Dark Ages and degraded religions.

PROFESSOR HUSKINS

Professor Toynbee's theory was, to say the least, regarded leniently by many American professors of history because, under the influence of Catholic pressure, they have, in recent years, gone so far as to deny that there was a Dark Age in Europe and have endorsed the mendacious Catholic estimate of the Middle Ages. Most of the men who do this are not distinguished in their science; though whenever I read their completely false accounts of the Dark Ages and the Middle Ages I recall with a feeling of irony the claim that is often made, that the professor is the only writer to follow with confidence when he remains within his own province. There is one, however, Professor Huskins of Harvard, whom I was surprised to find more or less in this shabby company. In his "Renaissance of the 12th Century" he says that—"the Dark Age means all that came between 467 and 1453." I doubt if there is one historian who brings the Dark Age beyond the year 1100, though naturally one may have escaped me. But beyond question European historians commonly make the Dark Age the period from 450 (or 500) to 1050 (or 1100). Yet Professor Huskins gives his readers to understand that these historians commonly make it last to 1550. It is, of course, then possible to point to the great art, etc., of the 13th and 14th centuries and ridicule imaginary writers for vituperating it. The longer period is not the Dark Age but the Middle Ages, as the Cambridge History and all responsible writers agree. In the circumstances I leave it to the reader to describe as he pleases this statement of the leading professor of history at Harvard and one of the most distinguished of American historians in our time.

SIR RICHARD GREGORY

The truth is that the number of historians who, under religious influence, have, in writing about the Christian period in Europe, made statements that are absurd in the light of the generally accepted facts, is as large as the number of professors of science who have similarly erred. When professors other than historians stray into the field of history they are apt to reproduce any sort of legend that favors religion or "law and order" (conservatism). I have recently pointed out such conduct on the part of two eminent British scholars (and, I may add, Rationalists). One is the distinguished scientist Sir Richard Gregory who, addressing an audience of Ethicists and Rationalists (in a Conway Memorial Lecture) and deploring the decay of character in our age, said ("Education in World Ethics and Science"):

"In the age of chivalry, of the 11th to the 14th centuries, duty to noble service gave refinement to the character of the warrior. Love, honor, loyalty, and piety were esteemed as major virtues, and courtesy, courage, obedience, and respect for women as minor."

That is, compared with the teaching of every leading authority on the period in all countries of Europe, the exact opposite of the truth. According to all these authorities the immense majority of both the knights and their ladies were erotic, cruel, callous, and dishonest.

DR. GILBERT MURRAY

In the same series of lectures—given to an Ethical audience, be it noted, and on a special occasion—Dr. Gilbert Murray, retired Oxford professor and one of the most distinguished Hellenists in the world, referred repeatedly to the First French and the Bolshevik Revolutions, and, in fact, to popular revolutions generally, in such language that he was clearly entirely ignorant of the facts. Of the European revolutions since 1798 he said: All revolutions are full of horrors and inhumanities. There have been about 40 such revolutions—the people winning freedom and democracy—and (clerical-royalist) counter-revolutions. In the counter-revolutions, directed by the clergy and royalists or dictators, more than 500,000 men, women, and children lost their lives and many times that number suffered in vile jails or in exile. In the actual popular revolutions—I exclude the Terror which was four or five years *after* the French Revolution and the Civil War in Russia that the Whites began nine months after the Soviet Revolution—less than 500 were killed, and there were no official reprisals. Dr. Murray as a great literary professor is not an historian, though history enters largely into his work. I give this for the consideration of those who so highly commend professors as guides. There are today few professors even of history who tell the full and objective truth about Christ and early Christianity, the Middle Ages, the struggle for democracy in the 19th century or the recent history of Russia, or discuss the causes of the second World War.

My own experience is that when a specialist professor—invaluable in his own sphere—steps outside it, as large numbers do, to pronounce on some other subject, he does not give one tenth the time and care to the study of it that the responsible "amateur" does. When it is a question of saying a good word for religion most of them seem to think no study at all necessary. Millikan, Compton, Conklin, etc., know well that the readers of their occasional articles on religion are unduly prejudiced by the weight of their authority on a totally different subject. What they say is usually a series of artless reflections that were examined and refuted in the last century or that betray a lamentable ignorance of the relevant facts. They do not show the least sense of responsibility when they throw out an expression of their profound admiration of the character of Jesus, the "unique" moral teaching of the gospels, the influence of Christianity in history, or the social influence of the churches today.

SIR E. RAY LANKESTER

Many years ago one of the leading British scientists, Sir. E. Ray Lankester, a Freethinker, was invited to contribute to a Rationalist annual. The editor told me that he sent in a paper on the "unique" ethic of Jesus which was as uncritical as a Baptist sermon. He sent it back to Lankester with a copy of a book of mine in which, after months of research, I had shown that there was not a single unique sentiment in the New Testament. Lankester sourly refused to be taught by me, and when the publication appeared and contained an article by me on "The Popes of the Renaissance"—in regard to whom I have read every contemporary document in Latin or Italian—he broke into the familiar censures of "the popularizer." I owe an incalculable debt to professors of science and history—it is their work I purvey to the public—but may ask them to recognize their limitations: 1) they rarely have either time or inclination to make a sufficient study of matters outside their particular field to express a useful opinion on them, 2) it is just as possible in 30 to 40 years—I have myself been engaged in this for 65 years—to get a sound general knowledge of all that is really pertinent to one's philosophy of life as it is to get an exhaustive knowledge, if you want it, of the anatomy, physiology, ethics, etc., of snails or the molecular texture of all known crystals.

As to the essayists, journalists, radio-spouters, and didactic novelists and dramatists, who shrink from no subject under the sun when it comes to talking but are little inclined to the serious study of anything, it will be enough to remind the reader that this book is about the dumbness of the "great." Tastes differ, but I would hesitate to apply that epithet to your Lippmanns and Winchells, to say nothing of the oracles who dictate the opinions of millions because they have glib or malicious tongues, skill in bribery, or the slap-dash style that suits folk who are intoxicated with jazz or swing and are incapable of serious reading. In this, of course, I do not include such men as Shaw, Aldous Huxley, Eugene O'Neill, Steinbeck, etc. Yet the pessimism and anti-science of these writers are, however different, as lamentable as the blunders of Schopenhauer, Butler, or Tolstoi. Even Aldous Huxley does not understand the science he belittles, while the conception of science which Eugene O'Neill has in mind, in "The Dynama," for instance, is as bad as a Fundamentalist's idea of evolution. Unfortunately their literary skill is such that everything they write is broadcast in the literary columns of the papers, which are mostly written by other literary men, or by neurotic speakers on the radio. Many men and women who ought to be doing what any man can do to rescue the world from its temporary misery and create a disgust of the callous influences which would make it peaceful by suspending atomic-bombs and poison-gases over it are driven into an unhappy silence in which they brood over a "mechanized" or a "materialistic" age, while they could not even correctly define those terms.

In the days of Amen-hetep III, of Aristotle, of Pliny, even of Leonardo da Vinci, the blunders of the great were honest blunders. We if we had lived then, would have shared them. The world was wrapped in a mist. The blunders of able men in our time are not of that pardonable character. There are few pragmatists today in the theoretical sense, but there is a vast amount of pragmatism. Vested interests, profane or sacred, are still powerful. A streak of mysticism in the temperament of a man who has not the time or the inclination to study what it moves him to regard as obscure still makes men go down on their knees and say that the sun circles round the earth. The chain of gold is still more baleful in our age of wealth. So we continue to wrangle with each other about old creeds, about the path the race ought to take if it is to avail itself fully of the beneficence of science, while the mist has cleared from every reality that matters. We pass on great problems—the nature of the brain-life we call thought and perception, the nature of the basic stuff of the universe, etc.—to the future. But a man's philosophy of life does not in the least depend upon the solution of these. The fight is won—in theory—as far as concerns the practical direction of activity, individual and collective; and this is for us the fundamental problem of the universe.

Absurdities of the Christian Religion

by

Joseph McCabe

CHAPTER I

THE CHILDISHNESS OF PRIMITIVE CHRISTIANITY

The Christian conception of human life, nature, and destiny is in its essential outline absurd and childish, and the weapon that it dreads above all others is ridicule. Its apologists have, therefore, in our time encouraged a distinction between two classes of critics: the polite, restrained, if not reverent Agnostic and the scurrilous Atheist. They fully recognize the rights of the one; because only a thousand or so—and they are rarely Christians—read him. They summon all the standards of our refined civilization to condemn the other and, wherever it is possible, invoke the police to silence him; because he has 10 readers to one reader of the courteous critic, and his work is more apt to unsettle the believer.

It is a psychological error to say that it is useless to ridicule the views of a man whom you would persuade to abandon them. Ironic, pungent, or humorously contemptuous writers have contributed most to the emancipation of the human mind. Medieval Europe was prepared for the Reformation by the discreet irony of Erasmus and the open raillery of Ulrich von Hutten; and Luther's broad and often coarse ridiculing of Roman priests and practices was far more effective than his appeals to scripture or the pedantic learning of Melanchthon and the sour severities of Calvin. Later the erudite and courteous criticisms of the Deists weaned only a section of the thoughtful middle class from Christianity, but the caustic raillery of Voltaire extended the revolt with great rapidity from class to class and from Madrid to Berlin and even St. Petersburg. Paine's sober irony opened the eyes of more Christians in England and America than did all the critical works that were published in half a century or more. Ingersoll's Mistakes of Moses penetrated pious circles which his most eloquent lectures never invaded. All but fanatics like a laugh.

We have, unfortunately, no Voltaire, no Paine, and no Ingersoll today Such writers as we have who can handle a witty or ironic pen are warned off this delectable field for satire. Once, lecturing on a Sunday in an Australian variety-theater and having to wait a few minutes in a dressing-room, I found myself confronted with this printed warning: "Don't say Damn: we don't care a damn but the public does." There is in the offices of editors of papers, and magazines an unprinted law that it is unprofitable to tell the truth about religion and a mortal sin to ridicule it, so the Great Illusion of its unique respectability and its profound influence is sustained. Let us look at it as people are looking at it in Russia today.

1. The Teaching of Paul

Many religious folk say that the Christian faith will regain its influence if it sheds all the clericalism, ritual, and dogma it has acquired in its passage through the Middle Ages and returns to its primitive purity. Some historians find it possible to please the godly by taking seriously this legend that 1,900 years ago a new and superior religion of great ethical simplicity appeared in the Greek world. These historians have clearly never studied either the content of primitive Christianity or the contemporary religions and philosophies to which they assume it to be superior. There was, in fact, no primitive Christianity. There were at least two very different new religions, with Christ as the central figure, and both were, in essential features, far below the level of idealism which the Greek world had already attained.

The first was the religion set forth in what are known as the Epistles of Paul. Since we are concerned here only with the ideas, we need not worry as to whether this Paul was a solar myth or a lunar legend or a fiery little Jew who, in the cosmopolitan city of Tarsus, where the sensuous cult of the Mother-Earth goddess clashed with Persian-Jewish puritanism, gave up his trade and joined the large band of wandering apostles. Whether he was a real person or not, there is behind his weird ideas a development that it is impossible to trace. A vast and priceless literature was destroyed by the Christians of the 5th Century, and in the little that survived we get only tantalizing glimpses of religious and moral developments between 200 B.C. and 200 A.D. of which it would be deeply interesting to know more.

Paul's teaching is not that men must be just, honest, kindly to each other, and so on. There was not a moralist from Persia to Spain who did not teach that. It is as old as the oldest Egyptian literature, and for centuries before Paul the cities of the Greek world had heard it all from philosophers and moralists who were often honored as the guides of entire cities; whereas Paul, if we take the Epistles as historical, never had more than a few dozen followers in the largest cities. And the smallness of his following was exactly due to the fact that the really new ideas—new, that is to say, to the Greeks—he brought along were stupid and revolting.

It is no use saying that this is quixotic or prejudiced. In spite of all the gorgeous praise of Paul that lingers in our literature, nine educated persons out of 10 will admit, at least privately, that the idea that God, conceived as a spirit equally infinite in power and goodness, keeps a place of torment in which billions of the weak humans he has created will suffer agonies for ever, is a revolting idea on the moral side and a childish idea from the intellectual angle; and that the further idea, that he condemned the whole race to this vast torture-chamber because the first human pair were guilty of a trivial and melodramatic act of disobedience, and that his "wrath" was averted only by some part or aspect or other childishly-conceived duplicate of himself becoming a human being and dying a horrible death, is for us moderns beneath discussion.

But that is exactly the personal teaching of Paul. In his Epistles the shriek about the wrath of God and eternal damnation, about how we all "died in Adam" and can escape only by believing in

Christ's atoning death and resurrection, almost drowns his preaching of the ordinary virtues; in which preaching he has no more distinction than any other moralist. Only on one ethical point is he more or less distinctive. All sexual-intercourse outside marriage, he thunders, gives you a ticket to hell, and even marriage is a grudging concession to weaklings, because sex is essentially loathsome. He is not original but Persian or Essenian in that; but it was new to the Greeks, and even his own followers (especially at one of their best centers, Corinth) smiled at it. Where he brought a really new gospel to the Greek-Roman world (true sources of it being now untraceable) was in this barbarically-childish story of a hell-fire God who threatens to torture billions of persons because two of them stole one apple but is "appeased" when his "son" sacrificed himself on a cross.

2. The Gospel Theology

This Jesus who saves the human race from the most horrible fate that the imagination ever conceived, this God-man whose earthly adventures ought to be of unique interest, is so sketchily and scantily introduced on his human side by Paul that some scholars believe that to Paul he was a deity only, like Mithra. There is, however, some reference to his earthly side in every Epistle. What is much more important is that the second Christianity which appeared, the Christianity of the gospels, knew nothing whatever about Paul's version. The contrast between epistles and gospels is so marked that, while one set of scholars prove from the epistles that Paul never heard of a man Jesus, another set prove that the gospel-writers never heard of a god Jesus. It is, in fact, very probable that the earliest version of the gospels did not. And when we further notice that at least the Jesus of the gospels never heard of this terrible curse of the race for apple-stealing for which he is supposed by Paul to have come into the world to atone, the story begins to be funny. In the gospels Jesus is a very jealous preacher who is so close to God that he is permitted to turn water into wine for folk in the last exhilarating phase of a Syrian wedding-feast, so the Jewish priests get jealous and have him put away by the Romans on a political charge. He clearly has not the least idea that he is carrying out a stupendous redemption. He sweats blood at the prospect of death. He dies with the despairing cry on his lips that God has deserted him. One liberal theologian has scandalized his colleagues by actually suggesting that Paul never heard of this Jesus of the gospels.

But if the gospel-Jesus does not stoop to the ethically barbarous level of Paul with his curse of the race and his blood-atonement, he does meet Paul on the almost equally low ground of a belief in hell. Attempts to prove that Jesus never taught the myth of eternal damnation show only to what lengths one is permitted to go in the religious world. You just say that when the prophet mentions "everlasting fire" he really means a sort of temporary discomfort from remorse over your sins, and, behold all the difficulties are removed. Still worse is the plea that these passages are not authentic. They are found in what theologians of every school declare to be the oldest and most reliable part of the records.

In fact, the whole story becomes meaningless if you deny this,

for the essential mission of Jesus in the gospels is not to teach
people nice social behavior but to urge men and women to sell all
they have—everybody to sell and nobody to buy, or, to sell knowing
that you are putting very serious chances on the person to whom
you sell—and sleep in separate beds because "the world" was coming to an end within that generation. Lives of Jesus are being
written in America today by liberals who profess to meet our modern knowledge and spirit. Yet they represent as the supreme genius
of the race and the most elevated moral teacher of all time this
supposed prophet who fierily adopts the lowest conception of a God
—a hell-fire God—that any civilized nation ever entertained, and
who, while astronomers at Alexandria were measuring the sun and
its distance, clearly knew no more about the structure of the universe than did the dullest clodhopper in the valleys of Judea.

'These dominant ideas of the gospel-Jesus make his ethic socially absurd and mischievous. Before we even consider the teaching
attributed to him we have to swallow the initial absurdity of assuming that his remarks and sermons were taken down when he
delivered them and carefully treasured for 30 or 40 years until
they could be put in biographies. We know that there were stenographers at that time in Roman cities, but even the boldest modernist
seems to hesitate to ask us to believe that some Hebraic young man
with a roll of parchment or a waxed tablet followed the prophet
about like a modern reporter dogging President Roosevelt or Greta
Garbo. And that these supposed speeches were not written down
within 20 or 30 years after the supposed death of Jesus is quite
clear from the fact that Paul, who several times overcame his re-
pugnance to his fellow-prophets at Jerusalem sufficiently to go there,
never heard of them. By a remarkable feat of sophistry theologians
persuade their readers that Paul's pupils were not interested in
the earthly life of God—one would think they would bristle and burst
with questions about so remarkable a life—so he gave no details in
his Epistles. But even apologetic sophistry could not make us entertain the idea that Paul's disciples would not care to hear the
actual words of Jesus if he knew any. He never gives them. Are
we to suppose that Peter and the other organizers of gospel-Chris-
tianity passed the word round that this fellow Paul or Saul was
not to be shown any of their literary treasures?

Well, we overlook all these absurdities. We set aside Paul's
revolting idea of a curse of the race and blood-atonement as a
muddy Cappadocian current flowing into the pure stream. We ignore
the miracles as playful ebullitions of pious hero-worship, like Sunday School stories about George Washington. Then we consider im-
partially the unique, the sublime, the transcendent message treasured by primitive Christianity. And the first thing we notice is,
as I said, that it is framed in an expectation of a speedy end of the
world and flames for the majority of the people in it, which makes
it as suitable for our time as a Maori war-song would be. If we
succeed in ignoring this framework, we find it is, at its best, just
a collection of moral sentiments which were common to decent folk
all over the earth and had been for ages. Thales had uttered them
600 years earlier. Meng-tse had developed them on genuine social
lines long before in China. Rabbi Hillel was teaching them at this
time in Jerusalem. When we ask for the unique bits, we are supposed to go into ecstasy because Jesus said, "Suffer little children to

come unto me" (which, in less stilted language, is said to be a
sentiment or more than one Chicago gunman), or "Thou shalt love
thy neighbor as thyself" and "Love your enemy" (which are borrowed from a 500-year old Jewish book). For a long time it was understood that Jesus was at least original in the severity of the sex-
restrictions. Christians do not seem to have minded them very much,
but we now have theologians begging 'us to believe that Jesus never
meant anything so childish and reminding us of the character of
some of his associates and lady-friends.

3.   The Fusion and Confusion

We will return to many of these interesting points in our im-
partial examination of Christianity as it is presented to us today.
Let us first finish with the primitive Christianity to which we are
advised to return. For the origin of this there had to be a fusion
of the eccentric ideas of Paul with the quite different ideas embodied in the gospels, and the result was a glorious confusion. I
take it that in the first half of the 2nd Century copies of a score
of "gospels" (including those that were suppressed in the 4th Century) and about two score "epistles" and "acts" were in circulation.
Then a number of educated Greeks, in a recoil from the stupidities
of popular Greek mythology and hectic Syrian mythology and practice, were attracted to the new religion and thought they could make
something of it. The result was a blazing fight in every Christian
center in the Greek world. The men who tried to rationalize the
chaos of statements were called Gnostics, and the struggle between
them and the bishops, who scorned the idea that any further explanation was needed, was much less dignified than the struggle between
rival bodies of Theosophists a few years ago.

The Gnostics were suppressed, and the gospels and epistles
were taken together as the documents of primitive Christianity. You
just picked out of the mixture whatever suited you. If you were of
the pale, nervous, terribly serious type you hung on to Paul, regarded nine-tenths of your fellow-citizens as cursed and doomed to the
flames, and luxuriated fiercely in the blood-of-Jesus atmosphere. If
you were a eupeptic Greek of Corinth or Miletus, you selected the
passages in which Jesus "ate and drank with sinners," preferred the
amiable Mary (there is no ground whatever even in the gospels to
say that she was a converted prostitute) to the industrious Martha,
made wine at feasts, and so on. If you were a proletarian, you
treasured all the maledictions of the rich and the parable of the
workers in the vineyard. If you were a small capitalist, you quoted
the praise of justice, the command to respect authority, and the
parable commending the steward who made his money grow.

There is just one of all the gorgeous epithets bestowed upon
this message of primitive Christianity which I find justified: its uni-
versality. It suits everybody. Ministers read the same words of Jesus
today in Fifth Avenue churches and in the poorest parishes. The
same words were read to Louis XIV and George III: to the slave-
owners of Virginia and the slaves. They are read to soldiers in
camp, and to pacifists in holiday camp: to the professional prostitutes
in Mexican and South American towns and to nuns in their convents
in Massachusetts: to the Tammany leaders in their New York chapel
and to the Polish slaves in their Catholic chapels: to politicians in

Washington and Christian Socialists in Philadelphia. And nobody turns a hair. There is certainly something remarkable about them. They are the most remarkable mixture of moral platitudes and fanatical impractibilities, of counsels of gentleness and blood-curdling assurances of divine wrath, of puritan and anti-puritan sentiments, of the best social counsels of the age and the most immoral and degraded dogmas, that you will find in religious literature.

All this talk about a return to primitive Christianity is blah. The men who use that language have not the least idea of reviving it. They ignore the most characteristic things in it: the belief that one must practice virtue to escape hell, the praise of poverty, the sacrificing of one's opponents as "broods of vipers" (which in those days was the equivalent of calling them sons of lady-dogs), the praise of celibacy and of deserting one's family, the complete indifference to the greater social evils of the age, and so on. Then our Bruce Bartons select the sentiments that are left and are deliciously unaware that they were commonplaces of social literature from Spain to China.

As to the claim that there is something majestic, unique, tremendously impressive in the way these ideas are put in the gospels, the answer is simple: for the reasons I have given they cannot possibly be the words of the Jesus of the gospels, and therefore they are just the literary efforts of scores or hundreds of totally obscure Greeks who probably mended sandals or baked bread in Alexandria or Antioch. When a man tries to rebuke me by pointing out how many literary men have called them sublime, I retort by pointing out that all the writers and scholars of Christendom for 1,000 years said that a Christian scheme which had as its leading features such abominations as the curse of the race, the torture of hell, and bloody atonement was a sublime religion and far superior to any other known; and that it is singular that the writers who today discover the gospel-story to be sublime (Noyes, Chesterton, Sheila Kaye-Smith, etc.) choose it as it is presented by the Church—the Roman Church—which still insists that these abominations are essential to it. In the religious atmosphere you can see anything—and say still more.

CHAPTER II

THE CHRISTIAN IDEA OF GOD

Desiring above all things to be scrupulously fair and not to imitate the example of the servants, of God who shamelessly travesty and misrepresent our ideas, I set out to ascertain very conscientiously what the Christian conception of God is. There seems to be a quite general opinion that, whether God is or is not a myth, the Christian religion brought to the world a new and purer and intellectually superior conception of him as compared with that of all non-Christian religions or philosophies. But when one asks what this conception which is so definitely superior to that of Plato or Plutarch, of the best Egyptians and Persians, is, one's difficulties begin. One begins to wonder, in fact, whether nine out of 10 of these writers who so emphatically declare the Christian idea of God superior to all others could write three lines on the idea of God of Pythagoras, Plato, Ikhn-Aten (the heretic king), the Parasees, the Serapians, the Hillel school of the Jews, the Essenes, or the Mithraists.

But the chief difficulty is to agree upon the Christian conception itself. If I, being a very simple-minded inquirer, choose the conception of God which is presented in the New Testament, is firmly and plainly embodied in the ritual of both Catholic and Protestant Churches, and is accepted and treasured by four-fifths of the folk who still call themselves Christians, the cultured Christians whom I know or read tell me, derisively or patronizingly, that I am deceiving my readers. It appears that some 200,000,000 Christians agree with the Pope, whose conception of God still is (as I have shown elsewhere) that he demands that any member of the Church who honestly ceases to believe in him must be—or ought to be, if a wicked world did not thwart pious intentions—burned at the stake and then tortured for all eternity. It appears that some 200,000,000 other Christians rather think the Pope ought to be burned at the stake for wanting to burn them, but agree with him that God tortures for all eternity, say, our high school boys and girls who in the heat of summer or of the dance embrace each other too ardently. But it appears that we are expected to take no notice of these 400,000,000 Christians and their beliefs and concentrate our criticisms upon the conception of God of the few million who are left. It then further appears that these have so many different conceptions of God that you might as well talk of "concentrating" on a whole stage-full of Ziegfeld girls. So we will just take three typical forms: the Moral God of the small educated minority, the Immoral God of the immense majority of Christians, and the Metaphysical God of this majority and of the ritual.

1. The Sky-Father

Advanced Christians and stuck-at-the-past Christians like Alfred Noyes and Dr. Riley, Papalists, Lutherans, Henry-the-Eighthists,

Calvinists, Baptists, Congregationalists, etc., all agree that Christianity introduced and teaches the highest known conception of God because it presents him as the father of all men and as all-holy and the guardian of morals. Sometimes they venture to put it that Christianity was the first religion to teach that God is Love. Which seems to call for a new definition of "love." The God of the Old Testament had been a sort of Semitic Adolf Hitler but he had at least let men pass into a vague sort of rest when they died and had not had a pit of fire ready for the majority of them. You really ask a lot when you ask us to say that the New Testament, which introduces original sin and hell and human sacrifice as a scapegoat for sin, converts Jehovah from a God of Wrath to a God of Love; not to mention that Christians so interpreted his new character that in the next 1,500 years there were more religious wars and more millions of people sacrificed for religion than there had ever been before.

We have the same difficulty in recognizing the beauty of the name Father, but, we will not linger over this because there was not the least originality about it. Not only the God of the religious Stoics was the father of all men, but the chief God of all Greeks and Romans—Zeus-pater and Jupiter—was in his very name the Sky-Father, or the Father in Heaven. In fact, the Sanscrit name of the chief God of the Hindus being the same (Dyaus-pitar), the one deity of all peoples from Armenia to Crete being the Mother of all men, and the Jews being perfectly familiar with the idea that Jehovah was their father, it rather looks as if the early Christians adopted a popular phrase, instead of inventing a new one, and tried desperately to make it fit what was really new in their conception of God.

At all events, the apologist says, wearily, Christianity gave the world its first ethical and all-holy God, and that was a terrific aid to morality. We do not want to be too punctilious, but as a matter of fact all the gods I named in the first paragraph of this section were ethical gods. The Osiris of the Egyptians had been a stern ethical god and judge of men on at least as high a code of morals as the Christian for more than 3,000 years, Shamash, the guardian of justice in Babylonia, for 2,000 years, Ahura Mazda, the sternest of all ethical gods, in Persia for 1,000 years, and so on. And when the good apologist says that the general acceptance of the Christian God in Europe—even if it was in most cases with the point of a legionary's spear at your buttocks—was a terrific aid to morals, we submit that that point ought to be settled by facts rather than by elegant reasoning. The truth is, as I showed in the last essay, that the substitution in the mind of Europe of the all-holy Christian God for all the earlier gods was followed by the worst and most prolonged degradation that, as far as we have clear knowledge, ever occurred in history.

Just one other point. When we are told that the Christian God was the guardian of morals, and we ask how in that respect he differed from the Sky-Father of, say, Aeschylus or Plato, the Manicheans or the Mithraists or the Serapians or the Jews, Essenes, Therapeuts, Mazdaeans, etc., we are told that he not only insisted, like these, on justice, truthfulness, honesty, etc., but he brought a new, rigorous sex-law into the ancient world. We will not waste time in asking whether even in this he was really any different from Ahura Mazda, Serapis, or the deity of Pythagoras, for this simple reason: the new sex-law was a transcendental superstition or tabu which, as such, has no value for the modern world. We moderns really do not want a principle which would persuade our women to become nuns and fancy themselves superior to other women. The Christian conception of sex, as such, is morbid and absurd, and it has led to an enormous amount of hypocrisy and suffering.

2. Savagery of the Hell-Fire God

Naturally, what we have so far seen does not make the Christian conception of God itself absurd. The absurdity here is in his apologists who claim originalities and superiorities and practical consequences which are ridiculously untrue to the facts. But we are examining Christianity, not the pale and fantastic version of it which a minority of liberals offer us. If, indeed, these liberals or modernists were gaining ground so rapidly that we might suppose that before long all Christians would hold a Christianity like theirs, we should have to take them more seriously. But they are not. Atheism has, as I have shown, won at least 100,000,000 adherents in the last 15 years. I doubt if all the liberal and modernist organizations in Europe and America have won anything like 1,000,000. Therefore, Christianity is still the religion of the Hell-Fire God and must be treated as such.

I have not much to add to what I have already said about this, but let us get four points clear. One is that it is quite the lowest conception of God that has been presented by any religion since the beginning of civilization. It is worse than the old Phoenician cult that demanded human sacrifices, because the pain even of the parents whose children were sacrificed lasted only a few years. It is worse than the Hindu cults which encourage men to torture themselves, since the poor dupes wear themselves out in a decade or two. It is worse than the degenerate forms of Buddhism which come nearest to it with their horrible hells, because in further Asia the idea of torture, however unsound, was supposed to be in the social interest, whereas in nearer Asia, in the environment which provided the pre-Christian roots of the Christian hell-idea (unless you prefer to regard it as a special revelation), torture was mainly a sheerly vindictive weapon of princes and nobles. The ethic of it was not that it was preventive, or not that alone. An injured or insulted monarch was supposed to vindicate his majesty by inflicting torture on the offender. That was the Christian idea.

The second point is that religions like the degenerate forms of Buddhism which have hells never appealed to the educated Chinese or Japanese. Even their priests were, and are, no scholars, and their followers are the uneducated millions. It shows the pernicious influence which these ideas had on the whole Christian scheme that scholars and saints and poets were completely reconciled to the idea of hell. All those marvelous geniuses of the medieval Church, from Aquinas and Scotus to Bellarmine and Suraez, proved that the hell-fire doctrine, in its purely vindictive sense, was thoroughly sound and just. Great artists like Dante and Michelangelo accepted it as cheerfully as they accepted the myth of angels and archangels. In short, the whole string of divines from Augustine to the 19th Century said that it was perfectly just, and the bulk of them let it be believed that they hold this today. Every saint in the calendar and every learned man until modern times accepted it. Yet apologists want us to believe that there is no agency in the world better fitted to give delicacy and soundness to the moral sense than the Christian religion.

I have already said that this perversion of the judgment of even the ablest men for centuries by their religious beliefs excuses us from taking the least notice of the claim that a belief held by many men of distinction cannot be absurd and must not be ridiculed, so we pass to the third point. It is that this barbarous doctrine not only did not work from the ethical standpoint, for there was more vice and crime in the most Christian period than there is today, but it caused an appalling amount of suffering. Jurists defended the barbarism of law until the 18th Century on the analogy of God's treatment of offenders. Tolerably decent men and women suffered agonies from fear that they might incur the terrible sentence. Relatives of dead men and women who had abandoned their creed or had died, after gay lives, without religious ministration, were racked with grief.

Finally, the moral enormity of the idea is increased when you reflect that the Christian God is supposed to have made men and women what they are. Apologists try to get out of the difficulty by inventing. one fantastic quality called "free will" which God gave to everybody and another called "grace" which he was prepared to give to all who asked for it. We need not discuss them. The Christian idea is that God directly or indirectly created a race of human beings and foresaw that in point of fact the majority of them would so behave that he would damn them. Presumably he knew as much about astronomy as Sir J. Jeans does and therefore knew that this race would last for 100,000,000 to 200,000,000 years, so the victims would run to billions. I am, of course, not counting the prehistoric races because they were lucky enough to live before Adam and Eve ate that apple, which was, on the strict data provided in the Bible by the ages of the successive patriarchs, only about 6,000 years ago. And whether these Acheuleans and Mousterians and Aurignacians incurred sentence of hell by their own sins, the learned theologians have not yet informed us.

3. The One-Three God

Liberal Christians will protest that the intellectually fantastic doctrine of the Trinity must not be put to the score of Christianity. The doctrine was, they say, fabricated in the 4th and 5th Centuries, at a cost—they don't say this—of some tens of thousands of Christian lives and enough passion and hatred to run a major war. It was then the universal Christian belief, obligatory under pain of death, until the 17th Century. It is still the firm belief of nine Christians out of 10 apart from the Unitarians and perhaps the Congregationalists. It is enshrined with honor in the articles and ritual of all the greater Churches, and it was shown to be perfectly reasonable by all theologians from Augustine to the professors of American Catholic universities today.

Perhaps it is not for us to say whether this makes it a Christian doctrine or not, but we may point out that the whole muddle arose inevitably from the essential religious drama of the New Testament. The poor Greeks and Romans had a hard time getting the story clearly. God was very angry with the world and doomed the whole race to hell until God became a man and atoned for men by a painful death. Who, precisely, atoned to whom? Many of the Greeks said that, since the new religion admitted only one God, he must have atoned to himself, and there was as early as the 2nd Century a shriek that these Patripassians were heretics. They were so muddle-headed as to confuse God the Father with the God in Jesus, simply because they were told that there is only one God. However, the Hebrews had been wont to call very good men Sons of God, and, of course, every pagan knew that Zeus or Jupiter had plenty of sons, so there was the formula—if you cared to quit thinking. For those who wanted to understand it, theologians showed beautifully how the Son was "engendered" by the Father, though they were both the same age, and then a Holy Ghost "proceeded" from the Father and the Son, though he (she, or it) also was of the same age, or eternal. There were not merely aching heads for three centuries over this, but they broke each other's heads in hundreds of fights, even archbishops squaring up to each other and monks using their staves very lustily.

And at the end of all the tumult of the fighting, which (on Christian principles) might all have been avoided if the "clear and simple" gospel of Jesus had contained a few words about it, the Christian mind perceived at last that God had three persons and one nature and Jesus two natures and one person. This, of course, makes the Christian conception of God far superior to that of the Jews, the Platonists, the Parsees, or the Mohammedans. But I fear I may get really frivolous if I linger any longer over this mystery, so we will pass to a consideration of Jesus.

CHAPTER III

THE PUERILITY OF THE JESUS-STORY

To say the truth, mere lay Christians have never claimed that the doctrine of the Trinity made the Christian conception of God intellectually superior to any other. When they examined it closely, they almost always fell into heresy, as Sir Isaac Newton did. But their religion was essentially, for all Christians until modern times and still essentially is for the vast majority, a belief that Jesus was God yet atoned for the sins of men, so the paradox had better not be contemplated too long. Newton ought to have known that human genius could penetrate the secrets of the solar system but should not aspire to understand everything in a religion which was bringing new light to the erring and deluded race.

Passing over therefore all the attempts that have been made from the time of St. Patrick onward to persuade us that if there can be three leaves in a shamrock or three sides to a triangle there can easily be three persons in one nature, let us examine the story of Jesus. In Church and Sunday-School libraries there are very moving works of fiction about life in the early Church, telling how some pagan Greek or Roman reads for the first time one of the gospels and embraces at once the beautiful story of a God taking on human flesh and living amongst men to help and redeem them. Somehow St. Augustine's letters, which I had to read in order to write a life of him, did not give me that impression. Though Rome had fallen and the temples were closed or destroyed, he complains that the educated pagans politely smiled at his Christian story. Paul says that the Greeks pronounced it "folly." However, relegating these noisy modernizers to our last chapter, let us examine the story of Jesus for ourselves.

1. Its Morally-Depraved Basis

The first difficulty is that, as I said in the first chapter, there are two different stories. Paul says that Jesus was a God whose redemption of the race by dying on a cross so predominated that Paul would not even mention his moral teaching and his miracles. At least the God in Jesus did not die or suffer at all; though how there was an "infinite satisfaction" to the Father—he being infinite, a sin against him, the theologian says, is sort of infinite and requires a sort of infinite expiation—when only the finite part of Jesus suffered, I am not in a position to explain. However, the gospels, as we saw, though written long after the epistles, know nothing about this. Lots of men worked miracles, even raised the dead, in Greek as well as Hebrew literature, without needing to be Gods. But when one interpolation in the gospels after another enhanced the supernatural character of Jesus until he became in some sense God, this earthly career of his got more and more puzzling. What the dickens was a

God doing in that galley at all? Or words to that effect. Paul gave the explanation. God, who had cursed the world and had furnaces ready for most people in it, so loved the world that he sent his only-begotten son to redeem it.

The modernist gloss on this is not Christianity but an acknowledgment that Christianity has been wrong in its vital principles for 18 centuries. It is itself too feeble even to replace Christianity. It says that Jesus came or was sent to teach men—and he did not teach a single thing except hell and the end of the world that was not being taught by the Hillel school in Jerusalem and in every Greek city—and to set a good example—which was so beautiful that nobody thought of writing a description of it until about half a century later. Then, having exaggerated to the nth degree the very ordinary virtues ascribed to Jesus in the gospels, and omitted all the cursing and sweating blood, etc., these modernists, who say that he came only to show us a model of virtue, find that he had an immensely larger share of God in him than the rest of us have, so he could no more help his virtues than we can help our weaknesses.

However, we will come back to them in the last chapter. Jesus as the founder of an ethical-culture society is one thing but Christianity is the cult of Jesus as a God. And Paul's explanation why God became human is the only possible one and is, in fact, the belief of the immense majority of Christians. It is a farrago of crude primitive ideas. God makes Adam and Eve and is supposed to know exactly in advance what they are going to do. His omniscience tells him that the chief consequence of his making of man will be that he will have to damn at least 1,000,000,000 mortals a century to ferocious punishment for at least 100,000,000 years.

You will observe that I am not here carping about the childish way this is put in the Bible: how God was walking one day in the garden and noticed that a fruit was missing from a tree in the fenced-off part, and so he fell into a towering rage. . . . No, it is not simply this that we find absurd. This is just a pretty little bit of folk-lore like Bluebeard. What I am reflecting upon is the teaching of the Church, or all the Churches, as refined and rationalized by the great theologians like Aquinas and Suarez, who even (the apologists say) anticipated the principles of the American Constitution, and Luther and Calvin. God could not be angry, of course. The prayer-book and hymn-book and Bible and all the rest that talk about the wrath of God merely mean that with an infinite coldness and passionlessness he created a human race for which, he foresees, he will have to make torture-chambers accommodating about 100,-000,000,000,000 souls; and if the same beautiful drama is being enacted on all the planets of the super-universe. . . .

But we will omit conjectures and stick to the official teaching which, being read out if not preached upon in all Catholic and Protestant churches every Sunday, must be part of the well-known soothing and uplifting quality of such services. The official story then runs that the majesty of the passionless God was so outraged by Eve's peccadillo that death alone could atone for it. You might think that so great and independent a God could just please himself whether he wanted any atonement at all and that being so loving a God, he might just laugh it off or put Eve across. . . . . It is terribly difficult not to make scurrilous remarks here. However,

theologians, who know all about it, say that there had to be atonement or else God was compelled by his own loving and holy nature
to damn this human race he had created. And since no mortal was
important enough to make the atonement, one of the personalities
of the one God had to select a carpenter's hovel in a very obscure
part of one of the tiniest globes in the universe and become Jesus.

All this is not childish, because to say that would be an insult
to children. It is ancient oriental monarchism in its worst form
blended with pre-civilized ideas like that of the scapegoat and the
expiatory sacrifice. The basis of the whole story is immoral.

2. God Plays on the Streets

But the story becomes childish in its next chapter. An ovum in
the womb or the oviduct of a village-carpenter's best girl is miracu-
lously fertilized and develops normally until the hour of parturition.
Then, so that the lady may remain a virgin, the fully-developed baby
passes—At any rate, it is born, and Mary retains the treasure of her
virginity. We may say for the writers of the gospels that they did
not impose this story upon their readers. It was the Fathers of the
Church and those wonderful theologians of the Middle Ages who
worked up this version. The gospel-writers simply said that Jesus
was one of the children of Mary and Joseph who somehow or other
was found after 30 very ordinary years of life to have some sort of
unique relation to God.

However, we will not be tempted to stray from the official
Christian teaching, which even some university-professors and large
numbers of college-trained folk listen to every Sunday with rapt attention. They do not see the puerility of it because the gospels
which described the infancy and boyhood of "the divine child"—
telling how he used to crow over his pals by making clay pigeons
and turning them into live pigeons, and so on—were dubbed "apoc-
ryphal," and the Pope tried 1,500 years ago to suppress them all. This
infancy and boyhood of Jesus are so very unpleasant to think about
that the Church retained only those gospels which skip (except for
one episode) from the circumcision (which is explained away to
little girls in Sunday Schools as an ancient Jewish rite the nature
of which we have forgotten) to the 30th year of age. In fact, many
theologians would like to get rid of this indelicate section of the
doctrine of the incarnation by supposing that God united with the
man Jesus only at his baptism by John or at his transfiguration.
But that is heresy or at least modernism. Our 30,000,000 Fundamentalists, including Catholic professors, teachers, writers, statesmen, etc., believe that the little mite crawling about the floor in a
Nazareth 'dobe cottage 1,900 years ago. . . .

But we won't imitate the wicked Voltaire and pry too closely
into the infancy. One fancies, in fact, that an educated Catholic or
Methodist does not spend much time imagining Jesus playing about
the village-streets or learning his father's trade and . . . I had
better refrain again from dwelling upon it all. I have heard thousands of sermons in my time, but, hard put as preachers are at times
for a new theme, I never heard one who ever said a single word about
the life of Jesus as an infant, a boy (except where he beat the learned men in the temple in argument and told his mother to mind her
own business), a youth, or a young man in his '20's. It is amazing

that people of education should still be found who believe the pre-
lude of the story—the doom of the race, need of atonement, etc.—
but at least they seem to acknowledge, implicitly, that any serious
reflection on the life of the man-God up to the age of 30 would be
dangerously disturbing. It certainly ought to be. Just that section
of the Christian story, of which every Christian fights shy, will seem
in another 100 years so extraordinary a piece of mythology that the
psychology of the believer will be considered one of the most ab-
struse of problems.

3. Evading the Police

If you ask why it was not arranged that all this very trouble-
some business was not avoided by having the incarnation at the age
of 30, as the modernists more wisely arrange it, several pretty reasons are given by theologians, but the real reason why the Churches
stick to the old doctrine is that, if you go into detail, the life of
Jesus from 30 to 33 is almost as baffling as the earlier period. Of
course, we will not go into detail. When George Moore did it (The
Brook Kerith), the theologians of London wanted him sent to jail,
but he was too distinguished a writer for the police to interfere with.
So I just leave to the imagination the details of the life of a workless
and homeless wanderer, with a few rough fisherfolk who went about
with him. But you must remember that he is supposed in all these
vicissitudes and experiences to be, in part, the power that created
the million galaxies of the super-universe.

It is bad enough to reflect on the story—the "simple and sublime"
story—as it is told in the gospels and rationalized by the theologians.
The idea seems to be that before he sacrificed his life to make the
great atonement, Jesus was to make an impression on his generation.
Theoretically, he could have been like Mr. Wells's invisible
man, or could have told the Lebanon range of mountains to throw
itself into the Mediterranean, and so on. For inscrutable reasons
he let his power leak out so feebly and ambiguously that no one
thought the events worth writing down until, half a century later,
a citizen of Tarsus came along and won a few hundred "followers of
Christ." In fact, some theologians now say that in the actual gos-
pel-narrative there is nothing supernatural at all. For instance,
when it says that a few loaves and fishes were so multiplied that
they fed thousands, it means that when the disciples brought these
few loaves and fishes out of their bundles and offered to share them,
everybody else was moved by their example to produce their hidden
lunches and offer to share. But that is a weak-kneed concession to
modern science, and the enormous majority of Christians, whose belief we are examining, insist on the dear old miracles.

In fact, if you cut the miracles out of the gospels and you then
remember that the speeches also must be forgeries unless you
prefer to believe that there was a staff of stenographers and that what
they took down was thought so unimportant that it was pigeon-holed
for half a century, the only miracle left is the extraordinary paltri-
ness of the record of a god moving about amongst men for three
years and the way in which he put their backs up. He seems to be always running away from cities, which he apostrophizes from a safe
distance with a "Woe to thee" (which is the Hebrew way of saying
"Blast you"), and then getting great crowds of peasants together

in obscure places which are obviously totally unknown to the writer of the gospel (since he just says "on a mountain" or "in a desert place"). The feud with his mysterious enemies thickens. Sometimes they are represented as the Wall Street men of Judea, a small body of rich and very hypocritical men called Pharisees; though in point of fact, the Pharisees were at that time the great body of the Jewish nation, including workingmen, who strictly observed the Jewish law.

So the story—remember that this is the cosmic, the most thrilling event, of all history, the saving of the race by a god-man—runs on to its climax. One of the little group double-crosses the world's redeemer (who must have known from the start that he was going to do so) in some way. The meaning of this must necessarily be that Jesus, after melodramatically asking his men how many knives (poetically called swords) they have between them, decides to dodge the town-guards by sleeping out in an olive-orchard beyond the walls, and Judas gives him away. In a final miracle he sweats blood —the greatest theologians have explained that that is quite possible —when he sees the police coming, and then the Jews play their pre-destined part in the glorious redemption of the race by putting him to death; for which the good Christians, who alone were redeemed, rob and revile and murder the Jews unto this day. There is really something to be said for the Jews because Jesus, according to the gospels, was so silent to the end about the world-redemption he was accomplishing that the modernists can plausibly claim that he knew nothing whatever about such a thing. He first asked God to forgive his executioners on the ground that they acted in good faith; in which case there was nothing to forgive, and in any case somebody had to be the executioner in the divinely-ordained sacrifice. Then he bitterly complained that God had deserted him, and finally, though he was God himself, he asked God to take care of the human soul with which he had been blended for 30 years.

We will not go on to reflect on the resurrection or the miraculous transformation of the corpse into a live body which could pass through stone and brick-walls yet could eat dried fish and walk; or on the very remarkable statement that the god-man, even in this glorified form, could saunter along the country lanes (presumably stopping at every wayside pub) with a group of his old companions and be mistaken for just a hobo or a jobless carpenter; or on the final moment of this extraordinary career when he stood on top of a hill and sailed out into space in the direction of the Polar Star. We will just be content to say, with all respect to the learned professors and writers, the shrewd businessmen and still shrewder politicians, who accept it, that this official Christian teaching, shared by all but a small minority of our 400,000,000 Christians, is puerile from beginning to end.

CHAPTER IV

THE THREE-STORY HEREAFTER

The essence of Christianity, in so far as it is really found in the New Testament, officially taught by the Churches, and conceived by the immense majority of Christians, is that God made men with immortal souls as well as bodies; that for their sins, inherited or personal, he condemned the great bulk of the race to some sort of eternal torment which was best conveyed to them by the picture of them burning forever—and the great theologians of the Middle Ages showed that it was quite possible for even souls to be thus grilled—in devil-tended fires; but that, having a triple personality, and being the God of Love, he detached one personality to blend with a human being, live for 33 years as a peasant's son lives in Mexico, and then suffer a terrible death to appease—well, presumably to appease the two other personalities. We have examined two of these propositions in the light of common sense and kindly feeling and now we turn to the third.

With its doctrine of an immortal soul that had a very definite location after death, Christianity certainly did bring something new to the majority of the Greeks and Romans. Like most of the peoples of antiquity, they had never bothered much about what happened after death. "I shall not wholly die, but a great part of me will escape the tomb," one of their poets had said; and the great Emperor Hadrian had, as he lay on his deathbed, composed a pleasant little poem to his soul—or what some philosophers called his soul, though he probably did not believe in it—which began with the question: "Pale and vague little soul, where are you off to now?" Apart from a few esoteric sects, they thought this soul just wandered about in a mist underground with no particular pleasure or pain. It is true that by the time the first wild and wooly Christians like Paul arrived, certain eastern religions had spread over the Greek-Roman world—chiefly Mithraism and Isisism—which also held very definite views about the soul and its future.

The prehistoric world had always, as existing savages show, been fascinated and baffled by this question of the after-death. Both their secular and religious authorities had found it very useful that they should believe that good and humble conduct would be richly rewarded beyond the grave. This helped to reconcile them to the smallness of the reward they got in this world. And it was a small step from this to say that the wicked would be positively punished in the next world, so we get hells here and there amongst barbaric peoples. When they rose to the level of civilization, the Sumerians and Semites rejected this belief as childish and took no interest in a life after death. The Egyptians clung firmly to the belief in an eternity of bliss for the virtuous, though they mercifully taught that the wicked soul which was weighed in the balance and found wanting in the Hall of Osiris was just dropped into the mouth of a

crocodile and annihilated. But, late in the development of civilization, certain hardy and truculent pastoral peoples came down from
the hills overlooking Mesopotamia and founded the Persian civilization: by the usual method of robbing every existing city after kill-
ing enough of the citizens to prevent resistance. From these very
religious Persians the Jews learned the idea of a definite future life
with rewards and punishments, and just at that time the Christian
religion appeared and, as it were, specialized on this peculiar doctrine which is so very soothing to the poor.

The Idea of the Soul

Thus the Christian belief that the New Testament contains a
"revelation" of the true destiny of man is as ingenuous as the belief that Jesus taught ethical sentiments which nobody else knew
at that time. It is, of course, an amiable weakness to boast that
your house is the cleanest in the street or the roses in your back-
garden are the finest; and, if you are sensitive about truthfulness,
all that you have to do is to refrain from looking inside your neighbors' houses or at their roses. So you can't accuse Christians of
lying when they say that the teaching of Jesus was unique and far
superior to any other teaching of the 1st Century, because they have
carefully refrained from studying the teaching of the more humane
rabbis, the Essenes, the Mithraists, the priests of Isis and
Serapis, and the Greek moralists; though you might perhaps not
uncharitably observe that when men of science like Millikan and historical writers like Durant and even certain professors of history
and philosophy repeat the popular superstition about the uniqueness
of the teaching of Jesus without comparing it with other teaching,
they ought to be brought before some academic court of honor.

On our present point it is quite easy, if you live in a city with
a good library, to learn that the Christian religion was not at all
original. There is an English translation of the sacred books of the
Persians, the Avesta, and on page after page of the oldest part of it,
written centuries before Christ, you read how Ahura Mazda would
one day be so angry about the sins of men that he would fling a
star at the earth and burn it up with the souls of all wicked men,
dead or alive, summoning the souls of the virtuous (especially in
point of sexual virtue, because the flesh had been created by the
devil) to eternal bliss. This last day the Avesta calls "the coming of
the kingdom," and in its pages the good Zoroastrian constantly prays
to Ahura Mazda, "Thy Kingdom Come." In other parts of the Avesta
it is described how at death the soul of each man and woman is
examined. The virtuous enter at once upon a pleasant eternity: the
evil go to a place of darkness: and there is even a third place for
the indifferent. So you get the complete three-story scheme of the
hereafter centuries before the time of Christ. I hope the phrase "three-
story" will not be thought flippant, because I borrow from the learned
British theologian, Bishop Barnes. If you have not the chance to
read the Avesta, see the articles in the Encyclopedia of Religion and
Ethics. There you will learn also that before the time of Christ the
Persians invented an intermediate god, Mithra, to redeem the souls
of men from the terrible wrath of Ahura Mazada, and he took flesh and
was born among men. This Mithraic religion, which the greatest
authority on it, Cumont, calls "essentially a religion of the lowly,"

spread much faster than Christianity did in the Roman Empire.

But do you and I really care two cents whether Christianity was superior to Mithraism or Stoicism or any other 'ism of 1,900 years ago? We do not go into raptures because the Phoenician ship was superior to the Cretan or the ladies of Athens were superior to the Phoenician. The question is whether this conception of the nature of man which more than nine-tenths, indeed in this case all, of our Christians hold today is superior to the conception of the nature of man which results from 100 years' intense study of man by psychologists, physiologists, and evolutionists. Not one in 10 of the masters of those branches of science believes in an immortal soul, and not one in 10 even of our philosophers accepts it in the sense of personal survival.

I have shown all that elsewhere and will here only observe that it accords very happily with our personal experience of life. We feel that there is something out of joint when our Christian neighbor says that Mussolini has sent 100,000 immortal souls with poison-gas and bombs for hospitals in Ethiopia or that immortal souls in Germany are hounding the Jews. We have misgivings even when we contemplate an audience of 15,000 souls watching a pugilistic show in Madison Square Gardens or listening to political orators. We smile when we look at ourselves in the glass or when, sitting over the fire with a drink from 11 to 12 at night in a New York room, we wonder fancifully what the 8,000,000 other immortal souls are doing or look like at that hour. . . . Enough. This idea of an immortal soul is an ancient superstition which modern psychology and the tracing of the evolution of man cause to look as childish as a totem-pole in a modern city.

2.   The Insipidity of Heaven

I have already said so much about the degraded character of the belief in hell that we will not return to it. We must, in fact, here acknowledge that Christians themselves are rejecting it in large numbers and it is becoming a joke of the comic theater. More than half a century ago divines of the Church of England began openly to reject it and, as that Church is under government control, the fanatics appealed for their expulsion. The appeal failed, and the witty comment of a famous British lawyer, "Hell dismissed, with costs," was richly appreciated everywhere. But it is Christian doctrine. It is the plain teaching of Jesus and Paul, and it is one of the most treasured and obligatory convictions of members of the three biggest Churches, Romanist, Baptist, and Methodist.

A wit called it "one of the consolations of Christianity," and your Christian friend will say that this at least applies to the doctrine of heaven. Does it? A professor once sent me a questionnaire asking whether I wanted to find the belief in immortality true. I replied candidly that I certainly did not want to find myself unable to cut my spiritual throat if I found myself after death in a new world with more boring conditions than this. Immortality under unknown conditions which we cannot control might be a curse. To my surprise, knowing how eccentric I am, the majority made the same reply to the questionnaire. And that is true of the great majority of men and women in any modern civilization. We write books on every imaginable theme today. It is even more important to say something new than to say something true. But I have yet to see the book or article which claims that any number of our churchless millions are in tears because they have lost their hope of heaven.

The truth is that nobody ever made the Christian idea of heaven look attractive. Dante dismally failed, and Thomas Aquinas, with his "beatific vision," just strings words together. Al Jolson lately had a film showing the colored Christians' heaven as an eternal Coney Island, but even that might fail. Some years ago there was a revue in London—I do not know if it was presented in America —one scene of which boldly depicted heaven as a sort of Central Park with perpetual summer and light costumes in which you met all the most charming sinners of history (Nell Gwyn, Nelson's Emma, etc.) in eternal freshness. That looked better. But when censors pass these things, the old superstitions have become jokes. Candidly, men don't want to live for ever with their wives or with the ladies who carried prohibition, and by all accounts these will be in the majority in the Golden City. Besides, there was until lately the redeeming feature that before long the soul would be happily reunited to the body, and then the fun would begin. But these Jeans's and Eddingtons have put back the Last Day and the Resurrection for about 200,000,-000 years, and it's a long time to wait for a drink. I forget the title of Mark Twain's skit on heaven, but that is what the modern world thinks about it.

3.   The Gold-Mine of Purgatory

A Spiritualist medium who was a Jew once very kindly put me into communication, through the ouija board, with the soul of a German Catholic theologian who had died some time before, and the soul and I had an interesting conversation. In the end I asked: "Where are you?" "In heaven," he replied. "Then," I said—to the soul, of course, not to the medium (who, however, blushed), "you're a damned fraud, because on every principle of theology you ought to be in purgatory." You see, Jews know nothing about the Catholic doctrine of purgatory, which is a sort of mezzanine floor to which they are not admitted in the post-mortem building, and, since I have many Jewish readers, I must explain.

I have said that the old Persian idea was that the world and the souls in it would one day be purified by fire. That, of course, was only one of the ways in which, as the Father of the Church Firmicus Maternus said, the devil tried to delude the heathen by anticipating Catholic doctrine for them. It was Jesus and Paul who told how the sinful soul which has repented and escaped hell must nevertheless be purified by fire before it can be admitted to heaven. So purgatory is a temporary hell. If you have read Dante's Purgatorio, you must understand that the man is in that part of the Divine Comedy not a sublime exponent of Catholic doctrine, as is so often said, but a vile heretic, a precursor of the modernists, who basely tries to accommodate the doctrine of purgatory to human reason. It is reasonable enough without taking all the virility out of it. The Catholic who dies after a priest's ministrations or, if there is not time for these after at least saying—it may be only mentally— "I'm sorry," cannot go to hell. But we are all sinners and have to be cleansed before saying Good Morning to Peter at the gates. And the cleansing is so very hot that it need not last long for the average decent person; though, for instance, a prostitute run over on the street but who has just time enough to say "Sorry" or an Irish or Italian gunman. . . . Well, you understand. Their souls need polishing up a good deal before they are admitted to the Golden City. So in its unique mercifulness and tenderness the Catholic Church has decided that certain words in "the simple message of the gospels," which everybody else understands in a totally different sense, mean that there is a place of temporary punishment as well as a place of eternal punishment. It has until modern times always been represented by Catholic writers and theologians that the punishment is by fire, and the official hymn for what is called the Feast of All Souls (in purgatory) still runs:

> Pray for the holy souls that bur-r-n
> This hour amidst the cleansing flames.

I leave it to the learned theologians again to explain how spiritual souls are grilled in flames and why the souls of sinners who have just scraped through are "holy," but the Church has not officially pledged itself to the belief in material flames.

Still there are a few aspects of this "clement doctrine" which puzzle the simple-minded inquirer. The doctrine of hell is plain enough. If, for instance, a boy and girl about 10 years old have been pulling each other about improperly on the way home from school—it is said that this sort of thing occasionally happens—and have been run over and killed instantaneously, of course their little souls go to hell for all eternity. God is Love; and all the refined Catholic mothers and daughters, all the artists and literary men and scholars of the Church, say that this is quite just if not loving. But suppose the two little sinners have time, before they die, to murmur "Sorry," or if there happens to be a priest on the footway and he waves his hand in their direction and says "I absolve," then it is sound theology that the sin is forgiven. And in that case further punishment is sheerly vindictive. The need to make their souls holy before they can enter heaven could be met, and much better met, by Sunday-School classes with the angels as teachers. No, it is not at all a nice doctrine.

But I will tell you what it is—it is one of the most profitable religious doctrines that was ever invented. St. Peter's and the Vatican Palace at Rome were practically built out of 20 years profit on it. The rescuing of so many millions from hell by inventing purgatory for them did not suffice for the maternal tenderness of the Church. Its next step was to discover ways in which the purgatorial sentence passed by God could be shortened or remitted. The ribald outsider with no imagination fancies that he sees a difficulty in this judging and passing sentence on each individual that dies. If there are thousands of inhabited globes in the universe, there must be at least hundreds of mortals dying every minute, and some of the older ones must have a very long and interesting dossier in the celestial archives. . . . But this is all nonsense. To an infinite mind this simultaneous and instantaneous judging of 1,000 persons, spread over some quadrillions of miles of space, a minute is as easy as creating or annihilating a universe.

No, the real difficulty is to understand why God passes, say, 1,000,000 purgatorial sentences in a year, knowing that practically all of them, in the case of Catholics, will be shortened. The answer is that he desires the Church to accumulate great wealth to do its work in the world effectively. 'The Holy Ghost which guides the Church, as we shall see in a moment, inspired it to formulate the doctrine of indulgences; though why it used chiefly for this purpose Pope John XXIII, whom it later inspired the fathers of the Council of Constance to declare "addicted to the flesh, the dregs of vice, a mirror of infamy . . . guilty of poisoning, murder, and persistent addiction to vices of the flesh" and a few other things, I do not pretend to know. However, John's development of the doctrine of indulgences was retained in the Church and further developed.

The original idea had been that when a man went on a crusade or made a pilgrimage to Rome, so much was taken off the purgatorial punishment he would get when he died. Then an ingenious Pope found that if you gave the money to the Church instead of spending it on a trip to Palestine or Rome, you got the same benefit. This was what John XXIII developed. Why should only the rich, who could find these large sums, have the privilege? The price was lowered gradually until it fell to two bits, and then the millions rushed in. Friars like Tetzel went all over Europe, hoisting the Papal banner in the Churches and boosting indulgences like patent medicines. Dioceses and provinces were farmed out to the bishops or ruler, who paid, say, $50,000 down. Sometimes, as in Spain and Spanish America, which kept this singular custom until our own time, the local church sold the indulgence-papers through the booksellers, and the Vatican merely got 10 to 20 percent. But no guarantee was given with either partial or plenary (full) indulgences, so you kept on buying and trying.

The other chief branch of the trade, if one may use so secular a word for something so sacred, was to have "masses" said or sung for the dead person. Again there was no guarantee, so, according to your means, you had 10, 50, or 100 masses said, at from $1 to $50 a head. The priests of America today make something like $100,000 a day in this way. Then medals, rosary beads, holy pictures, and for rich people, relics, all loaded with indulgences, are sold in great quantities and at about double the cost of the material. So the doctrine of purgatory proved a veritable gold-mine, which the Church continues to work with very great profit all over the world. But in an age like ours, when you have not only to live but to bribe journalists and politicians and French statesmen and expend enormous sums in checking the inroads of Atheism, no one will be so churlish as to scrutinize too closely the principles on which the Church conducts its financial operations.

CHAPTER V

A HOLY GHOST WATCHES THE CHURCH

A Spanish author, Federico Urales, lately sent me a copy of an admirable work, La evolucion de la Filosofia en Espana, which he has just published. Running over the last part, in which he contrasts the progress made in our humanitarian age with the stagnation of the earlier religious period, he asks this very striking question: "What would God have done without man?" When so many people are asking what man will do without God, it is refreshing to find an author turning the tables in this fashion. But the Churches themselves ought to have raised that question. Let me explain that paradoxical statement.

There is a very admirable movement in our time for the reunion of the Churches. Down to, perhaps, half a century ago one half of Christendom described the other half as seduced by the Scarlet Woman or dominated by the Beast of the Apocalypse. But these Protestants were themselves divided, and the older Protestant Churches—Anglican, Lutheran, etc.—regarded the Methodists, Baptists, etc., as negligible riff-raff or Churches which ought to be content with the colored folk; just as the Roman Catholics regarded the Greek Catholics as degenerate orientals with a very doubtful chance of salvation. In fact, one branch of the Methodists regarded two other branches as traitors to the Word of God and not respectable. But they are now drawing together: not, of course, because they are all losing ground and had better pool their resources, but because it is not really Christian to be thus divided. The snag up to the present is that the Church of Rome understands by reunion the sort of union which the wolf made with the lamb, but when, in the fullness of time, its Fascist supporters are crushed and Socialism is established in Italy, Spain, and Austria, it will be in a more chastened mood. Long before the end of this century there will be a reunion of the Churches.

Then, I take it, the members of the Churches will say with my Spanish friend: "What would God have done without man?" For all the Churches, holding that the New Testament is the word of God, have to say that God, or the third part of God, the Holy Ghost, promised to guide and control the true Church, and each of them is the true Church. There was a division of labor in the celestial family. Personality No. 1, the Father, undertook creation and the guidance of life during its 1,500,000,000 years of blind and bloody stumbling upward until 1,900 years ago. Personality No. 2, the Son, then had a much shorter but decidedly unpleasant spell of work. Personality No. 3, the Holy Ghost, next had to begin and to act through the Church until the end of time. How all this was done and what came of it we must now consider, because, to put it in a word, the Church fell into a most unholy mess and confusion until our atheistic age set in and man, with his plans of reunion and pacification and rationalization, lent a hand.

23

1.   The Real Founders of the Church

It is said that feuds have at last died out in Kentucky, but those were simply quarrels about mundane matters and could not be expected to last as long as quarrels about more important sacred matters. The Church-world is still split by the great feud which broke out between Peter and Paul nearly 1,900 years ago. The Protestant Churches follow Paul, the Roman Catholic Church follows Peter, and the Protestant-Catholic and Greek Catholic Churches follow their own inclinations. The Catholic Church says that all the others are fools because they admit that the gospels are the word of God and a true narrative, and in these gospels (Matthew, XVI, 18) Jesus says that he is building his Church upon and handing the keys of heaven to Peter alone amongst the apostles, and that from the 2nd century onward it was recognized throughout Christendom that the Roman Church was Peter's Church. Naturally, the early Christians being a very humble and democratic if not communistic body, it was necessary to give them a sort of monarch, and this high honor fell to Peter and his successors, of whom that staunch rebuker of evil, Pius XI, is the living representative.

To all of which the Protestants reply that not a single Father of the Church ever acknowledged that the Petrine Church, as they were willing to call the Roman Church, had any authority over other Churches, but that they always stoutly denied it: which is very peculiar if the reading of the gospel is so clear. I have shown in my history of the Roman Church that this is perfectly true, and that the supposed quotations from the Fathers and Councils with which Catholic apologists support their claims are shamelessly garbled. Most Protestants now go farther and say that Peter never went near Rome and had nothing to do with its church; which seems to imply that all the Fathers blundered, but the Catholic apologist does not care to press that point. What is worse, many of the Protestants now say that some crook in the Roman clergy invented the story of the special choice of Peter and interpolated it in the gospels.

You will certainly find it interesting to read the 16th chapter of Matthew, which is the basis of the Catholic as distinct from the Christian faith. It says that the Pharisees (who were really more than half the people of Judea) and the Sadducees (who never had anything to do with them and would not have crossed the street to listen to a wandering preacher) came to ask Jesus to perform a miracle to prove his divine mission. Well, here was his great opportunity, since we are told that he spent three years trying to convince men that he was from God; and, after all, the Jews have been cursed ever since for rejecting one who is supposed to have made his mission perfectly clear to them by miracles. But, strangely enough, the gospel-writer calls the request a temptation of Jesus (who usually scattered miracles as casually as burnt match-sticks), and he tells us that Jesus called them hypocrites and adulterers and fools. It is a very great pity the talkies had not been invented at that time so that we could see and hear the creator of the super-universe telling the Pharisees in rich Aramaic what they were sons of. However, Jesus then asked his disciples who they thought he was, and, though he had been with them two or three years and wrought countless miracles, only one of them, Peter, knew. Not only does that seem to excuse the ignorance of the Jewish people

generally and make the curse of the race seem rather harsh on the
part of a loving Father, but—it gets curiouser and curiouser like
Alice's Wonderland—Jesus got them in a corner and forbade them
to tell any of the Jews that he was really the Christ.

We must say that this is not a very impressive document to be
made the foundation of the towering claims of the Papacy. Protestant theologians could have made mincemeat of the chapter long
ago but, unfortunately, the same critical mincer would then have
been applied to other chapters. However, the promise to Peter is
even worse than the rest. It strains that feeling of respect with
which we always handle religious matters to find Jesus calling the
most respectable of the Jews bastards because, a day or two after
he had fed 4,000 people with seven loaves, they courteously asked
him to show them a miracle, and to find the creator of heaven and
earth getting his companions together like a bunch of boy scouts in
a dark corner and swearing them to secrecy. But when it comes to
his making puns. . . .

Thirty years ago we British Rationalists used to have jolly
little dinners in London, and I would not have been surprised if my
genial old friend, George Jacob Holyoake, had, in the late and mellow
stage of one of these dinners, said to Edward Clodd, who succeeded
him later as our chairman: "Ted, thou art Clodd and upon this Clod
I will build the Rationalist Press Association." It is upon a pun of
that sort that the power and wealth of the Roman Church have been
built. Everybody knows the passage, "Thou art Peter (Rock in
Latin) and upon this rock I will build my Church." After this it is
a small matter to observe that there was no word in their language
for "church" at that time, and that he had repeatedly said that they
must not have temples or synagogues or priests or services. The
Greek word ecclesie which we translate "church" meant at that time
—as did whatever Aramaic word Jesus is supposed to have used—a
public meeting and would not suggest to any Jew's mind anything
remotely resembling what was later called a church and certainly
nothing that you could build on a rock.

So it looks to me as if the grand basis of the Roman system is
the tawdriest bit of crude popular literature that one can imagine;
but, of course, when I think of the tens of thousands of college-
trained men and women, including professors and authors, in America who take it seriously, I feel there must be something wrong with
my eyes. They would doubtless tell me that in that hole-and-corner
talk Jesus really told his disciples all about the marvelous organization which would be established in the course of time, but the sten-
ographer of the group lost all his (or her) notes except just the
fragment which would set the various branches of the Church aflame
against each other from the days of Pope Victor (190 A.D.) to this day.

We may prefer here to agree with the Protestants, who say that
some Petrine rogue interpolated this passage in the gospels, and
that the real account of the origin of the Church is in Acts. It seems
that things were very dull for a time after the death of Jesus. The
disciples were still, after three years' intimacy (and in spite of all
the secret instructions about the Church), as hazy about the meaning of it all as the Pharisees, for, when Jesus came to them after
his resurrection, they asked him if he was now going to "restore
again the kingdom to Israel": which, if we took these things serious-

ly, would justify the execution, since it shows that they were seditiously minded against Rome. However, Jesus hinted—it is one of his many miscalculations—that that would come in the course of time. He forgot to remind them that he had been telling them for a year or two that the end of the world was near. What he did tell them was that the Holy Ghost would take his place and guide them. And when he had added another stupendous miracle, the ascent into the stratosphere, to the resurrection, the number of his followers rose to the enormous figure of 120 (I, 15), and on the 50th Day (Pentecost) they received the Holy Ghost. But in spite of the fire and the new gifts of eloquence and miracle-working, the work went very slowly until, about 10 years later, Paul came in and put ginger into it. In another 20 years there were a score of "churches," with a score or two of followers in each, and Christianity was established. In 30 years it had made less progress than the latest colored prophet of Harlem made in a month.

2.   Its Holy Record

To this point I have courteously followed the Christian documents themselves, but if one asks, as little boys do, what really happened, the answer of an historian must be that very few other events in history are so utterly obscure as this most stupendous event of all time, in which two persons of the Trinity "came down" to cooperate. All that we see with the cold historical eye is that there are a few fragments of Christian literature (notably the letter of the Romans to the Corinthian Christians which is wrongly titled the Letter of Pope Clement) belonging to the 1st Century which evince the existence of small groups of Christians and of the activity of Paul but they never refer to lives of Christ or gospels or quote anything whatever from them. For my part I am inclined to think that at the root of it all there was some Jew whose name the Greek writers of the gospels turned into Jesus and whom they represented as "the Christ" or the Anointed One. When I get to the essay in this series in which I discuss Jesus, we will discuss the bearing on this of the very early fragments of a gospel that have been found lately in Egypt.

But first let us consider the record of this Christian Church which the Holy Ghost took charge of "to teach it all truth" and to "be with it to the end of time." If I have any Christian readers of this essay they will at this point fear I may lose my habitual courtesy. For it takes a very ignorant Christian or else a Roman Catholic today to believe that the record of the Church since the 1st Century has been quite creditable to the Holy Ghost. From the day of Pentecost, in fact, one of the outstanding characteristics of the new religion was quarreling about doctrine and the vigor with which the quarrel was conducted. There were supporters of Peter and supporters of Paul, Judaizing Christians and gentile Christians, and so on. If the holy and learned St. Jerome of the 4th Century tells us, as he does, that he and another holy monk ended their argument on some sacred point by spitting in each other's faces, well, we wonder. . . .

The guidance in the matter of morals was not much more efficacious than in the matter of doctrine. About the year 220 the African Father Tertullian wrote a most scathing account of morals in the Roman Church, and about 80 years later his own African Church was described by its leader, St. Cyprian, as being in an appalling moral condition. Indeed, the early Christian historian Eusebius had to explain in his Ecclesiastical History (VIII, 1) that God permitted the persecution of the year 251 to fall upon the Church because it had become comprehensively corrupt. We can therefore imagine what a job the Holy Ghost had when, after the conversion of the emperors, the shower of gold upon the churches brought millions of Greeks and Romans to them. But I told in the last essay what happened then and during the following centuries. All Christendom sank into barbarism, and by the 9th Century the state of the Papacy and the Roman Church, which was understood to be the headquarters of the Holy Ghost, was a parody of the word religion. A German emperor—and he was rather a gay bird—had to come in and help with the flat of his sword.

However, at last, says the Protestant, the Holy Ghost got busy again and inspired men like Luther and Henry VIII to make a reform. No, says the Catholic, it was the devil who now got busy, because the Church had become so holy under Alexander VI (and his six children), Julius II, and Leo X (sodomists) that he became alarmed. It is very puzzling, but at all events the Protestant Churches assure us that the entire Church had gone damnably astray for 1,300 years, since they say, in Article XIX of the Anglican and the American Episcopal Church:

"As the Church of Jerusalem, Alexandria, and Antioch have erred: so also the Church of Rome hath erred, not only in their living and manner of ceremonies, but also in matters of Faith."

Since these good Protestant Fathers very decidedly held that the Church of Constantinople had erred just as badly—it had perished by the 16th Century so they omitted it—they mean that for 12 or 13 centuries the whole Church was corrupt in living and in doctrine.

It is very much to be regretted that, in bringing back men's attention from these vanities to the word of God, they did not offer us any explanation of the silence of the Holy Ghost, whose guidance is so emphatically promised in the gospels, during all that long period. However, they intimated, the Holy Ghost was now at work, and England passed into the hectic days of Elizabeth and the Stuarts, while Germany and the other Protestant countries of the North fell into the savagery of the Thirty Years' War. So Oliver Cromwell and his friends discovered, in the light of the Holy Ghost, that the Anglican and Lutheran Churches had gone astray like their predecessors, and they, like the German emperors of the 11th Century, laid the flat of their swords upon consecrated buttocks. But the people said that they liked not this new Holy Ghost, who put them on the water-wagon, and the corruption went on and new incarnations of the Holy Ghost (Baptists, Methodists, Congregationalists, Mrs. Eddy, Billy Sunday, Aimee McPherson, etc) had to arise in successive ages. But we will not conclude that we have to add one more to the absurdities of the Christian religion. Such phrases as the Church of God, God's ministers, guided by the Holy Ghost, etc., are too utterly devoid of meaning, in face of this historical record, to be called absurd.

3. The Word of God

The Six Pillars of Wisdom of the Christian Church are God, Jesus, the Soul, the Holy-Ghost-guided Church, the Word of God, and Business Organization, and, since we cannot quarrel with the reality and solidity of the last of these, we have only now to consider the fifth. Here, unfortunately, we have not one, but 100, doctrines to consider. We have the Old Guard, or the Fundamentalists, who insist that even Genesis and the Song of Solomon (composed in honor of his 753rd wedding) are literally the Word of God. Rather, we have two schools even here; the Baptists, who say that if you think otherwise you are damned, and the Catholics, who say you can think what you like but you mustn't say it. At the other extreme we have liberals who want to make a sort of Bushido like the Japanese, putting choice extracts from the Bible together with extracts from the Avesta, the Book of the Dead, Shakespeare, Ella Wheeler Wilcox, Father Coughlin, etc., and making a new collection of "inspired literature." Then, they say, even your daughters may read the Bible without a blush.

What one may assume today is that the ordinary educated Christian who takes any interest in the serious literature of his own Church admits the broad story of the evolution of the Old Testament. By far the greater part of it is rubbish and a great deal of it is deliberate forgery in the interest of the Jewish priests; and any publisher in America who published a correct translation of 100 passages in the Hebrew text would certainly go to jail. These Christians profess to continue to take an interest in the Old Testament only because otherwise they confess that Protestant and Catholic Churches alike have made an extraordinary blunder in accepting it as the word of God; and the highest saints and scholars of the Churches have been as fully duped as the peasants. It is another proof of the demoralizing influence of the religious atmosphere.

The New Testament I reserve for a later essay; and in another later essay we will consider the fatuity of the enthusiasts who are finding support for the Old Testament in archaeology, on such grounds as that we now discover that there really was a land called Egypt and a city called Babylon. We do not care today what God said in ancient Judea or Alexandria, or if he said anything at all. The measure of the "inspiration" is in the history of the world for a millennium and a half. Man seems to be making a better job of the world-task.

CHAPTER VI

MODERNIZING THE ANCIENT MYTH

When we linger over these absurdities of the Christian religion many writers try to deprive us of our simple pleasure by insisting that we are wasting our time. From their language you would be apt to gather that nobody believes these things any longer, yet when you inquire you find that, as I said, four-fifths of the 400,000,000 Christians believe them very stoutly. What we have been considering is not whether God really took a rib out of Adam to make Eve, or whether the story of Noah and the Flood is true, or whether men lived for hundreds of years at one time. The doctrines I have examined are really three in number: that God the Father condemns unrepentant sinners to an eternity of suffering and at one time so condemned the entire race for a trival act of disobedience told in a story which is as ingenuous as a Bushman legend: that God the Son then became man, lived as a man, and redeemed the race by offering himself as a sacrifice; and that God the Holy Ghost then came upon the earth to guard the new religion and its ministers. This is held by all Baptists and Roman Catholics and most Methodists and members of the Episcopal Church, and the millions of Four-Square-Gospellers and Triangular Theists and other independent Roaring Buffaloes. We are very refined and cultured but we feel that it would be rank snobbery to talk about Christianity and ignore these 30,000,000 Ancientists in favor of a few million Modernists.

But we would be courteous to all men, and it seems just after giving five chapters to the Ancientists that we should devote one to the Modernists. The justice or wisdom of this could be disputed only if there were a prospect of the entire body of Christians exchanging their faith in time for that of the liberals. We saw in an earlier essay that scientific analysis of the religious future compels us to reject that idea. The old Churches are losing heavily all over the world, but the millions pass, not to more liberal Churches or branches of Churches, but to the outer darkness of churchlessness. And the reason is not obscure. Modernism uneasily confronts, or evades, an awkward dilemma. Its work is to put a new meaning upon ancient phrases and formularies. Does it mean that Jesus, Paul, and the gospel-writers really meant what Dr. Bowie and Dr. Parks say today? Or does it mean that Jesus and Paul, whom it urges us to continue to regard as the greatest religious and moral geniuses of the race, were half-barbaric and wholly foolish in their fundamental ideas and have to be corrected by Dr. Bowie and Dr. Parks? We are really not surprised that even a Second Adventist or a Holy Roller turns up his nose at either alternative. This, he says, is either priestcraft or priestgraft.

1. Alas, Poor Paul

And even this scurrilous person wins our sympathy, within

measure, when we glance at the new Christianity. The famous gathering of 300 American and British bishops at Lambeth in 1930, the last Ecumenical Council that the Holy Ghost presided over, made an end of the old doctrine of the atonement. "The Cross," it told the world, "sums up the struggle of love against evil throughout the ages." Of course, we charitably make allowances for the difficulties of the bishops. They had their right wing in the Church, the lean, ascetic, fanatic folk who won't, part with their hell (for other people) at any price, and a left wing, who mutter that if this has to be Christianity they will look elsewhere. So the bishops, whose clear uncompromising utterance of principles is of such import to the world, had to trim. But at least they did not mention the Wrath of God or Hell or Atonement, and they did say that the cross stood for the struggle of· love against evil, whereas every prayer-book they had represented the crucifixion as the triumph of the suffering of Jesus over the wrath of the Father. In short, Modernism won a sneaking right to exist in the Anglican and American Episcopal Churches. The Pope, always so clear and decisive in his utterances, had, on the contrary, not only blasted such sentiments out of his own Church but had, literally, struck a· gold medal, representing him trampling on the dragon of Modernism, in honor of his victory.

At all events, it is very decidedly the teaching of the new liberal Christianity that hell, original sin, and the atoning sacrifice to appease the wrath of God are crude and abominable errors which must be abandoned. But even the apologist who can translate the "everlasting fire" of the gospel-Jesus as "temporary discomfort" falls down before Paul's rugged insistence on Adam's sin and God's wrath and the blood of Christ. So Paul Must Go. In his purely ethical passages he has not a single sentiment that was not common to the Jews. Especially the rabbis of the Hillel school, and all other moralists of the age. He was essentially the apostle of the fall, redemption, and resurrection, and, if you want to be Modernish—I mean Modernist—you must be silent about these indiscretions of the youth of your religion. Of course, you can still say that Paul was the second greatest religious genius of the race, because Christians never read Plutarch or Epictetus or the Talmud or Seneca or Plato or the Avesta.

2. Correcting Jesus

The more courageous Modernist says, let Paul go to the geographical region of the other world of which he was the chief explorer, and let us hear no more of him. That condemns to the trash-basket nearly half the New Testament and the immense and enthusiastic literature which has been written on it since Augustine. But there are compensations. Paul was always rather apt to steal the stage from Jesus, and now the latter remains unique, incomparable, incomprehensible. This is the grandest work of Modernism. It humanizes Jesus without surrendering a particle of his unique splendor. At first the Modernists said that it made the splendor more dazzling than ever, because as long as Jesus was regarded as God or at all events so·closely united to God that they made one person, his words and acts fell rather short of the standard. As a man he rises. . . . But it would not do to say too plainly that they rejected the divinity of Christ, so they got on to the formula that there was a great deal more of God in Jesus than in the rest of us.

In which case he could not very well help his superiority, and the
long string of superlatives the Modernists apply to him come peril-
ously close to one of the most un-modern practices of the Christian
religion: the abject flattery of and grovelling before the deity. The
more decent a monarch (or any man who does something big) is,
the more warmly he resents such flattery and grovelling. You have
to go back to a fat fool like Louis XIV for one who really liked it,
and further back still, to ancient oriental monarchs, for princes
who sternly exacted it. Are we going still further back, or going forward into the ultra-modern future, when we conceive God as, in the
naughty words of Mr. H. G. Wells, "a venerable old man with a
beard and an inordinate lust for propitiation and praise."?

I have therefore read avidly half a dozen of the liberal or semi-
humanist lives of Jesus of the last 20 years. It is amazing what an
enormous amount they know about him. A scholar of the Protestant
Episcopal Church, Professor Wenley, says in his **Modern Thought
and the Crises of Belief** (160):

"The gospels contain 2,899 verses; and of these, only 100
furnish strict biographical details."

He does not mean that there are 100 authentic texts from the historian's point of view, because he later says that "we have no absolute certainty that a single saying in the gospels was uttered in
that precise form by Jesus himself" (p. 161), and that "the facts
necessary for the life of Jesus in the historical or objective sense
simply do not exist" (p. 163). So what Professor Wenley means,
after his careful counting and study of the verses, is that only 100
in the whole four gospels profess to give biographical details. Any
author will admire and envy th skill with which these 100 verses, or
about two and a half pages of the Bible, are worked up into 400-page
and even two-volume biographies of Jesus, selling at $4 to $5 a copy.

But, of course, the main task of one of these writers, if he is
appealing to us moderns, is to collect at least one page of beautiful
deeds or noble sayings to which there is nothing equal in any other
literature in the world. And that is just what they never do. Of
the 100 verses giving biographical details the majority talk like a
little girl writing an essay ("we went up a mountain," "we came to a
certain place," etc.), so it ought to be quite easy to put before us
those which exhibit the sublime character of Jesus. It seems, on
the contrary, to be mighty difficult. He loved little children (even I
do that), he protested against the execution of an adulteress (I very
decidedly would, and people are protesting every day against death-
sentences on women), and so on. In short, these modern biographies
of Jesus are like puff-pastry, with a mustard-spoonful of inferior
preserve in an inflated four inches of sugared flour.

As to his sayings, it is even worse. First the new Jesusists have
to disavow or ignore the quintessential ideas of the preaching of
Jesus in the gospels; that the end of the world is near, and people
must hurry up and get sober to escape hell. Next they have to ignore
the score of ways in which this dominant illusion perverts the moral
sense of the gospel-Jesus. You have to sell all you have (to somebody
who is safely booked for hell) and beg your bread. You must treat
your family with cold disdain. You must not even admire a woman
with a graceful figure or marry. And so on. These are not "counsels
of perfection" but illusions of a small-minded fanatic, whoever real-

ly said them. Then the new biographer either ignores or falsifies or
turns into amiable pleasantries all the violent language (in oriental
language, cursing) about his opponents. One of the ablest British
apologists of the new school, Canon Streeter, said on this point (The
Spirit, p. 363):

> "I must frankly admit that the one objection to the belief
> that Jesus was morally perfect which I have found it difficult
> to meet is derived from the apparently exaggerated severity of
> his language to and about the Pharisees, who, with all their limi-
> tations, undoubtedly stood, as a body, for religious earnestness and
> self-sacrifice."

Even Streeter has to tone it down by saying "apparently" exaggerated
—just liars, hypocrites, brood of vipers, whited sepulchers, wicked
and adulterous generation, etc.—and he does not see that the simple
solution is that these. things were written in the heat of the controversy with the Jews long afterwards.

In fact, this whole business of biography-making and Jesus-
glorifying is as alien from the modern spirit as is the grovelling before God and the talk about atonement for sins. Decades ago old
Bishop Du Bose, of the Protestant Episcopal Church, wrote (Turning
Points in My Life, p. 115): "Let us remember that our Lord taught
absolutely nothing new." Of course not; but every other Modernist
says that he did and then declines to tell us what it is. They pick
and choose from the New Testament documents without a shadow
of principle. They "make tarts from Dead Sea fruit," Professor
Wenley says, and "say to historians, For any sake, and in the name
of anything you hold holy, allow the probability, or at least the possibility, of our plea" (p. 227). With their successive discoveries and
re-interpretations, they remind us of the psycho-analysts of 10 years
ago, finding new complexes and new interpretations of dreams and
religions every month.

Let us cultivate our garden. All this stuff has no more real
relation to our tasks and problems today than it has to Relativity or
Quantum Physics. Its exponents do not hope to help us, but to help
themselves—to our cash-boxes. An absurdity can never give wisdom. A lie cannot inspire a sound reaction. We want the mind of
the race clear. This nebulosity must disappear from it, from every
part of it. We do not want to restore crosses to our magazine-covers
instead of bathing belles nor to substitute parsons for economic experts. Christianity, whether in its old robes or modern backless
dress or nudist, is doomed.

www.ingramcontent.com/pod-product-compliance
Lightning Source LLC
Chambersburg PA
CBHW052206170626
46812CB00004B/1674